WHAT OTHERS ARE SAYING

"I loved Creativeship. The fable approach Kelleher uses to create his message of a new leadership was captivating. It has been a while since I read a business book I couldn't put down. A winner!"

— Bob Brustlin, CEO, VHB

"Agility, innovation, and alignment are three essential elements of a successful business that Creativeship operationalizes. While telling an effective and compelling fable, Bob highlights principles that are also backed by our extensive research on human capital management best practices. A must-read for new or emerging leaders, as well as any business leader looking for a leg-up in today's boundary-less, highly connected, and ultra-competitive marketplace."

— Kevin W. Martin, Senior VP of International Operations Aberdeen Group

"If I'm going to read a novel, it won't be from someone who bores me. Good thing Bob Kelleher is anything but boring. In a landscape full of dry talking heads on employee engagement, leadership, and talent practices, Kelleher is a breath of fresh air and a truth teller, speaking with transparency, honesty, and street smarts you won't find in most thought leaders in the Leadership/Talent Management space. No one ties business results with talent practices as well as Kelleher – as evidenced by the innovating fable approach you'll find in Creativeship. I just hope there's a sequel..."

— Kris Dunn, Nation's Top HR Blogger
HR Capitalist; Fistful of Talent
CHRO, Kinetics

"When it comes to true insight, it takes an experienced practitioner to provide this version of the absolute truth. The constant rebirth of Creativeship could only have come from Bob, the master, and he finds a way to tell it like it truly is. In an era that morphs into a different reality every few years, evolution is the answer, or obsolescence defaults."

— Andrew Filipowski, CEO
SilkRoad Technologies

"Kelleher weaves his personal experiences with data and research for one amazing fable. Creativeship's lessons are powerful and long-lasting for leadership teams wrestling with how to sustain their business for continued success. This book powerfully reinforces the need to for businesses to shift their focus on purpose, employee engagement, high performance, innovation, branding, and globalization."

— Gerry Salontai, Current Strategist
and Former Chairman and CEO
The Kleinfelder Group

"As baby boomers approach retirement, we are confronted with a period of self-reflection of our career and our lives that is profound. Looking at our leadership legacy, we must not look back but rather forward. Our experience, stage of life, curiosity, and craving to learn creates an interface and engagement with the new workforce and our own family in ways that require us to think and act differently. Creativeship captures that moment in a profound fable that represents so many of us!"

— Deb Hicks, SVP of HR
Dana Farber Cancer Institute

"Creativeship is a fable that will remind you of the need to build both a sustainable workforce and business model. I appreciated its blended approach— a fable rich with data and resources. Kelleher rightly points out the need to tap the potential in people by engaging them in new and deeper ways. Creativeship reinforces the need to understand both the purpose of a business and the intrinsic motivation of its employees as the key to shifting great performances to lasting legacies of performance."

— Danroy "Dan" T. Henry
Chief Human Resources Officer
Bright Horizons

"Simply put, Creativeship is to today's business leader what The One Minute Manager was in the 1980s. Its concept is transformative, and Kelleher has introduced it using a brilliant combination of fact and fable. The story not only offers insight into the reflections of an experienced leader, father, and would-be retiree, it translates his reflections into key concepts that build a compelling case for shedding outdated applications of leadership and evolving into the world of creativeship."

— Tracy Burns, Executive Director
Northeast Human Resources Association

"Creativeship is a must-read for leaders wanting to position their companies for long-term sustainable growth. In this engaging, clever, and though- provoking parable, Kelleher not only explains what principles we need to follow to lead effectively, but also why. As soon as you delve into the book you'll realize the story is a great read, and the lessons are critical."

— Bob Nelson, Ph.D.
Bestselling author of 1501 Ways to Reward Employees and 1001 Ways to Take Initiative at Work, among other books

Creativeship

Creativeship

A NOVEL FOR EVOLVING LEADERS

BOB KELLEHER

WITH LIZ BATCHELDER

BLKB
PUBLISHING

*Again and always, to my lifelong best friend and wife Candy,
and to the world's best kids, Marissa, Brendan, and Connor:
you mean everything to me.*

CREATIVESHIP

A Novel for Evolving Leaders by Bob Kelleher with Liz Batchelder

BLKB Publishing
7336 SE Tibbetts Street
Portland, Oregon, 97206

Unattributed quotations are by Bob Kelleher.

ISBN 978-0-9845329-1-9

Printed in the United States of America

Contents

About the Author

Bob Kelleher is an award-winning author, thought leader, keynote speaker, and consultant, who travels the globe sharing his insights on employee engagement, leadership, and workforce trends. His first book, *Louder Than Words: 10 Practical Employee Engagement Steps That Drive Results*, has been a best-selling employee engagement book since its release in 2010.

Bob frequently appears in national media and publications such as CNBC, CBS Radio, Business Week, Forbes, *Training Magazine*, Yahoo, and *Fortune* as a commentator, writer, and editor. His practical approach and willingness to share best practices, coupled with his enthusiastic and passionate delivery, have proven to be a winning formula for audiences throughout the world. An in-demand industry and conference speaker, Bob has spoken to hundreds of thousands of attendees over the past 10 years, while also presenting to the leadership teams of many of the world's top companies, including Shell, TJX, SilkRoad, Prudential, Lawson, Unocal, Abbott Labs, Fidelity, Balfour Beatty, Wurth, Millipore, and The Centers for Disease Control (CDC). He has been recognized as spearheading various award-winning business cultures, based on building cutting-edge employee engagement programs and initiatives, and is the recipient of numerous leadership awards.

Before becoming a speaker, author, and entrepreneur, Bob was the Chief Human Resources Officer for several global companies, including a Fortune 400 global professional services firm. He has also held positions ranging from Executive Vice President of Organizational Development to Chief Operating Officer. He is the founder of The Employee Engagement Group (EmployeeEngagement.com), a global consulting firm that works with leadership teams to implement best-in-class leadership and employee engagement programs, workshops, and surveys. In addition, he has recently introduced the world's first cloud-based employee engagement resource center, The Employee Engagement Library.

Acknowledgements

When I set out to write my first book, *Louder Than Words, 10 Practical Employee Engagement Steps That Drive Results*, I did not have a goal to write a second book. Writing a book was on my 'bucket list,' and having written one, I was content to focus my energies on building my consulting business. But an amazing thing happened since the release of *Louder Than Words*: people REALLY responded to both the message and the messenger. *Louder Than Words* sold more books than I ever imagined, finishing as Amazon's top selling book on Employee Engagement during 2011. Clearly, it resonated with many readers, and I began to receive invitations to speak and share my experiences and insights with leadership teams and conference attendees around the world. It was during these speaking engagements that the idea of writing a second book crystalized. Meeting such a variety of people from so many industries sparked my curiosity, which was already heightened by my fascination with today's workforce trends: globalization; increased levels of employee disengagement; the emergence of purpose-driven organizations; the influence of Generation Y; technological advances; social media and mobile technology; and ongoing unemployment challenges.

I discovered that although I still believe that employee engagement is the "secret sauce" that can accelerate a company's performance, it is an outcome of something greater. I began to ask why so many outstanding companies with engaged employees, healthy profits, and respectable growth ultimately failed. Why? It became clear to me that engagement, along with profit and revenue growth, are only part of the puzzle – critically important parts, but not enough on their own to allow a company to sustain engagement, profit, and growth.

This "something," I believe, is the next step in the evolution of leadership, and is the subject of this book, *Creativeship*.

Employee engagement, profit, growth, and client satisfaction by themselves are not sustainable. Even solid and inspired leadership is no longer enough; we've all seen once-thriving companies led by very talented people falter if not fail outright. I've often defined leadership as distinct from management, which is concerned with things, data, and processes, classifying it instead as the ability to lead people, build followship, and make money. But I have come to realize that definition is archaic. What businesses need is Creativeship, a paradigm shift that encompasses leadership while taking it several steps farther. I've defined Creativeship as "the creation of great and sustainable cultures and business models."

I chose the fable approach to writing *Creativeship* because I believe its message is universal, and deserving of a broader audience than a typical "business book." After all, good leadership is akin to good parenting, and effective leaders share many of the same traits as effective teachers. While *Creativeship* is chock-full of usable business data, the "fable" format provides a refreshing alternative to business books full of dry facts and figures, and magnifies a message that is equally relevant for parents, teachers, public sector employees, entrepreneurs, and of course, those working in business. And for those hungry for more business-speak information, the book's appendix provides practical business take-aways and suggested resources.

As for acknowledgments, I have to start with my editor and friend Liz Batchelder. When I wrote *Louder Than Words,* my consulting and speaking businesses were still in incubation. But since my first book's release, my consulting and speaking businesses have matured to include a docket full of great clients, a staff of talented associates, and an ambitious travel schedule. Liz's encouragement, time management, patience, and amazing editorial and creative skills have kept us on track for this second outing. As testimony to her significant role in *Creativeship,* you'll note her name on the cover. Thank you, Liz.

Special thanks also go to my work colleagues, who lovingly tolerate my idiosyncrasies every day as we work together building our global talent management consulting business, The Employee Engagement Group. Thank you, Steph Hogan, my "VP of Everything;" you are the soul of the business, along with being my right hand in everything I do. Thank you, John Konselman, for being the brains behind our content and workshops — always ensuring that our already ambitious quality standards are exceeded. And thank you, Allan Benowitz, our VP of Growth, who represents courage and vision in pushing us to heights previously unimagined. I would be lost without the three of you supporting me every single day – thank you!

I'm forever grateful for my partnership with the Northeast Human Resources Association (NEHRA), in particular Deb Hicks and Tracy Burns, for always supporting me as both a colleague and a friend.

Special thanks go to all of my friends at SilkRoad Technology for helping to build our technology, and in particular to Flip Filipowski and Ed Vesely for their ongoing support of me, including asking that I participate in SilkRoad's Asian Talent Management Road Show. Some of the globalization themes in *Creativeship* were crystalized during my Asian travels.

I also want to acknowledge and thank all of my clients for believing in me, and in particular, those special clients who have been there since day one and continue to be both valued clients and friends. These include, in no particular order, Allen Marr, Robb Googins, Bill Rizzo, Jeff Baker, Darlene Perrone, Howard Cohen, David Jones, Bob Brustlin, Keri Kocur, Michelle Perry, and Eric Stastny. *Creativeship* is a blend of real and fictitious companies and characters – which also afforded me an opportunity to give a nod to some of you within the story itself.

To Tracy Burns, John Jackson, Gary Torosian, Michelle Perry, and Claire Mello, you are very special for your "above and beyond" editorial review and enhancements. And thank you to Cindy Kazen for both your review and support of *Creativeship*, along with your ongoing help in promoting its message. Special thanks also go to all who graciously agreed to read my transcript in advance and provide a testimony, as highlighted in the first few pages.

And as always, thank you to those family members who continue to support me, and in particular, my father in law Ed Johnson, who shows more interest in what I do than anyone else I know. To Mom and Dad, looking down from above, thank you for instilling in me (and my amazing siblings Hughie, Pam, John, and my late beloved brother Stephen), everlasting values. Though we didn't grow up with much, you miraculously made us believe we grew up with everything. You were the best!

I dedicate this book to the world's three best kids, Marissa, Brendan, and Connor, who continue to make me and mom proud every day — both for the choices you make and the young adults you have become. Many of the generational themes of *Creativeship* were seeded from watching how you and your friends communicate with each other, and observing first-hand how your generation is changing the world we live in. You have been amazing teachers for your dad to learn from. Words can never describe the love mom and I have for you. And Drew, what a great addition you'll make to the family!

Lastly, I owe everything to my best friend and wife Candy. You were there for me when I was 14, and continue to be there every day. I would be lost without your guidance, love, support, confidence, humor, and most importantly, your perspective.

Purpose

The tires of Joe's elderly BMW crunched on the gravel as he turned down the lane, heading toward his daughter's house. She had been pestering him lately to buy a hybrid or a fully electric vehicle, but he maintained a soft spot for his old car. It was one of the first tangible signs that he had "made it;" in his day, owning a so-called "luxury vehicle" signified success. He'd taken loving care of it over the years, and it was difficult to imagine trading it in even if it sometimes did cost a small fortune in parts.

He was on time, as usual, but suspected that Heather might be late. He was deeply proud of her accomplishments and the career path she'd taken with Beacon Communities, a residential management company matching affordable housing for those in need, but she had clearly not inherited his almost obsessive need for punctuality. Pulling up to her house, he found himself smiling as he remembered the 20-to-30-minute sessions he had spent when Heather was a kid in this same car, waiting for her to emerge from soccer practice or drama rehearsals. In those days, there hadn't been a smartphone to entertain him, so the radio was his only diversion.

As if on cue, his iPhone began to vibrate as he yanked the BMW's parking brake. For awhile he had used a standard ringtone, but once he realized that many iPhone users had the same one, he decided it wasn't worth the confusion. He'd been in a restaurant or a lobby too many times scrabbling for his phone before he realized it wasn't his that was ringing.

"Hi Dad!" Heather said. Joe could swear he heard an echo; knowing that she was probably just upstairs in her townhouse-style apartment reinforced the impression.

"Hi, sweetie. Guess you just saw me pull up?"

"Yeah. I'll be down in a sec. I've just got to finish some work stuff and throw on some makeup. You want to come in?"

It was a Saturday night, but his daughter was involved enough with her job to be "finishing some work stuff." He didn't doubt it was important. As much as her time-management tactics differed from his own, he felt a surge of satisfaction at her commitment. Her mother, Joe's ex-wife, Donna, had been much like their daughter in this respect. "They'll wait!" was a frequent refrain. And Donna had been correct about that – for Donna with her various fundraising activities, where her charm was in high demand, they *would* wait. Joe suspected it was the same for Heather, who had an almost scary ability to cut to the chase and get things done.

"If you're only going to be a few minutes, I'll just wait in the car," Joe told his daughter.

"Okay. I'll be quick. You should Google the *Washington Post* article about global warming while you wait – the new one, by Stephen Prince?"

Joe's smile broadened. "Okay, maybe I will. But I'm happy just sitting here and admiring the view." Heather, like her brothers, always expected him to be fully informed about whatever issues were foremost in their minds. Sometimes he teased them by talking about Reagan and Bush-era economics, and reminding them that they hadn't taken any interest in those issues, either.

Apparently Heather had taken his comment about "the view" to heart, however. "I know, I know. You think I live in the boondocks. I really do appreciate your coming all the way out here to get me. But seriously, look at that moon! And I really have to hang up now so that we can get out of here."

"Okey dokey," Joe said. "See you in a few minutes." He pressed "End Call" and then looked out at the moon. Heather was right – it was worth contemplating. Full and low on the horizon, and covered with the pockmarks that made people imagine there was a face there. The Man in the Moon. In the autumn light, it shone a dull orange.

"You and me, old man," Joe said quietly, lifting an imaginary toast to his counterpart in the sky.

Joe was retiring. He didn't relish being the star of his own party, but some folks at his new company had wanted to throw him a shindig, and the guest list now included a lot of old friends and fellow-travelers. *Shoot*, he realized. *I'll probably have to give a speech!*

It wouldn't be that difficult. As a management consultant with some 40 years' experience under his belt, Joe was not exactly a shy violet when it came to public speaking. Clearly, he would want to thank everyone for coming, and make a few jokes about putting himself out to pasture with some golf clubs. But sitting here in the comfortable environment of his old car, waiting for his smart, successful daughter to join him, he felt suddenly that that might not be enough. What, exactly, was he going to say?

The BMW's door was thrown wide. "Hi, Dad!" Heather said, leaning in to give him a big kiss on the cheek. "Sorry I kept you waiting. And thank you for coming out to pick me up! My car will be back from the shop on Monday, but I didn't want to miss this."

She'd managed to put herself together remarkably well. Her hair was damp but combed, and she'd put on a dress – which Joe knew wasn't her favorite form of attire. He had an odd moment where the significance of his retirement struck him at the same time as the memory of his three grown children when they were little. He could remember Heather in a pink, knee-length Easter dress, and her brothers – now 20 and 24 – in the funny, miniaturized formalwear that is a boy's lot when forced to attend weddings or funerals.

Heather seemed to have read his mind. She shoved his shoulder lightly as he pulled back onto the gravel lane that led to her house. "God, Dad, quit it. Nobody died! This should be fun for you."

Joe didn't answer, but a smile tugged at the corners of his mouth. He imagined it looked a bit wistful.

"I'm glad you asked me," Heather said, giving the shoulder she had just shoved an affectionate rub. "It's a big night for you, and I'm the closest one. And let's face it," she added wryly, "I was always your favorite child."

Joe chose his next words carefully. "It didn't feel right to invite your mom now that she's remarried," he said. "And the boys are off doing their own thing right now." One was in law school, the other in his junior year of college. Both were miles away.

Heather seemed to sense his restraint. "They'll all be glad to know that you're actually retired and taking it easy." They rode in silence for a minute, and then Heather spoke again.

"What are you thinking for tonight, Dad? Did you prepare a speech?"

Joe turned onto the highway, amused that his daughter had sensed his concerns. "I thought I'd offer some reflections," he said. "Nothing formal. Maybe I'll talk a bit about things I wish I'd had a better grasp on when I first started my career," Joe said, trying the idea out for the first time.

Heather had been fiddling with her phone for the first several minutes of their drive. Something about what Joe had said had caught her interest, and they had at least 20 minutes in the car together before they would reach Joe's house, where the party was being held. Joe noticed with satisfaction that she was putting her phone into her purse.

"What, specifically?" she asked.

Joe took a stab at the heart of what had been bothering him about the whole retirement-party thing. "Well," he started. Then he felt a need to clear his throat. He glanced at Heather's purse; the phone was still safely ensconced. "You know, I think I had a good career," he said. Heather kept still. Her purse was in her lap, with her hands clasped over it. Joe hadn't always felt that he had her full attention, given her addiction to texting, but he seemed to have it now.

"I had a good career," he said again, "but I think it could have been a great one." There was a moment of silence wherein

Joe felt his face flush. But then, light broke through the clouds.

"You want to practice on me?" Heather asked. The sound of Crosby, Stills, Nash and Young on the radio cut through the silence, making Joe feel slightly less awkward. He knew Heather liked CSN&Y too, if only because she'd been forced to hear "Ohio" a thousand times over the years.

"Yeah, if you really don't mind," he said. "I feel like maybe I've bored you too much with this stuff in the past."

Joe was staring at the road when he spoke, but he had a mental picture of his daughter's eye-rolling that was now playing on a constant rotation. Surprisingly, when he glanced at her, he saw not only patience but genuine interest playing across her face. Her phone remained dormant in her purse. And then she said, "Tell me."

Joe didn't know quite where to begin. In 1968, when he graduated college, he was part of a family of six. His parents couldn't afford to pay tuition for all of their kids; heck, they were still paying down their mortgage. Instinctively, he knew this wasn't a story that Heather could relate to. He and Donna had always strived to open up a world of opportunity for their own children, and so far the kids had done very well for themselves. So he started carefully.

"When I was growing up," Joe said, "the only thing that seemed important was making money and providing for family. Being part of a company that paid well, and offered good benefits, because the role of the Dad was to be a provider. Long term, the goal was to 'get the gold watch.'"

He snuck a glance at Heather. She was listening, but the last phrase was clearly Greek to her.

"If you retired under the old arrangement, that was part of your send-off," Joe clarified. "A gold watch. You know, a tangible thing that meant *job well done.*" She nodded, and met his glance. He felt encouraged. "When I got out of college, I was so focused on making money," he said. "I didn't care how or what it was that the company did, or why we did it. You have to remember, I grew up with next to nothing."

Heather's phone rang, with some ringtone that Joe suspected she'd chosen herself and probably paid for (it certainly wasn't one that had come bundled with his own phone). Rather pointedly, she pulled it out of her purse and silenced it. Knowing that somehow, inexplicably, he had her full attention, Joe seized the opportunity. It didn't have much to do with the speech he had halfway formulated for his retirement party, but he surged ahead anyway. He'd always had his best ideas in brainstorming sessions with his team; this didn't really seem much different.

"I've actually learned a lot from your generation," he said. "From you, as an individual – your work with Beacon is inspiring. And also from your brothers," Joe said, as he saw Heather about to demur. "They're both interested in the larger purpose behind the companies they work for. Take Eric's job, in particular."

Heather sighed. Joe knew that, as a go-getter middle child, she disapproved a bit of her younger brother, Eric. Eric had changed his major three times at college before settling on graphic design. Although he hadn't yet found a position in his chosen field while he completed college, Joe was proud of the one-off jobs in Web design that Eric had picked up through acquaintances, and knew that he was one of the stars of his class. Heather had been eager to leave home, but Eric was content to live with Donna for the time being. Although he paid rent and had his own lodgings over the garage, Heather still managed to occasionally lord her own "independence" over her brother.

"Well, he's working for Whole Foods, as I think you know," Joe continued, "and when I walk into a Whole Foods, do you know what I see?" He didn't wait for her to answer. "They've got a short, catchy version of their purpose up there for all to see, that ties their customers in with the people they're serving. 'Whole Foods, Whole People, Whole Planet.'"

He paused, assessing his daughter's silence. She was regarding him evenly, clearly not yet "sold" on his endorsement of her younger brother's place of employment or sure where it might fit into Joe's speech at his retirement party. They had a long drive ahead of them, and given that this was the night he was meant to celebrate his retirement (with no "gold watch" likely to be handed over), he was in a speculative mood.

"I hope this doesn't sound like babble," he said. Heather was still looking at him without contradicting, so he charged ahead. "It's just that… in the past five years, I feel like I've finally gotten a handle on purpose, and why it's important for a company."

Heather seemed to sense a need to break the serious tone that had intruded on their commute. She made the same intake of breath – almost a snort – that used to infuriate Joe around the dinner table when they had all lived under the same roof. "What's so different about the past five years, Dad?"

she asked. "I mean, aside from your having to get back into the job market after ThinkSmart's whole downsizing deal."

"We lost our moral compass," Joe said. He was surprised at how easily the words came to his lips. He'd never confided in anyone about the doubts that had plagued him about the company he had helped build. It had taken being laid off from a top position with ThinkSmart to make him reflect on where the company might have gone wrong. But the very effort of putting his thoughts into words seemed to help verify them. And his daughter was the perfect captive audience.

"Look, you know what happened," Joe said. "I mean, in the most basic sense, we stuck with clients who were making decisions based on short-term profitability at the expense of other people's livelihood. And that was just wrong. It came back to bite us in 2002."

"Dad, I know," Heather interjected.

"2002 was when *everybody* knew," Joe continued. This was a simple statement of fact; the financial institutions that ThinkSmart represented had plummeted in that year. From Joe's point of view, ThinkSmart had got caught up in the profit madness right along with their clients. The record-setting 32% growth from 2000-2005 had everyone a little bit crazy; it had seemed that the bubble could not burst. However, "Things were wrong for a while before that," Joe told Heather. "We were part of the same short-term benefit trap as our clients. So in a way, it's only fitting that they took us down with them when they failed. Because…" here Joe stopped for a second, putting together a distressing thought. "It was all about accumulating wealth. For ThinkSmart, and for me. But… I think we've now seen that the pursuit of wealth alone is never sustainable."

This conversation wasn't helping Joe to put together any inspiring remarks to share at his retirement party. In fact, he felt a bit glum, and Heather's silence wasn't helping much. He thought she might actually be regarding him with distaste, which was not what he'd hoped for. He started to scan the radio; Heather's neighborhood was a bit out of range for his usual stations. And truth be told, he missed the old knobs and dials of the radios of his youth. He hadn't quite caught up with newer car stereos' intricacies.

"You mentioned Eric, and Whole Foods," Heather said over the static. Immediately, Joe turned the volume down. "You know," Heather continued, "much as I want to hate Starbucks, Raina is really happy working there." Raina was one of Heather's childhood friends, who was cranking away at a graduate degree while working as a store manager at Starbucks. "Their whole mission statement thing is similar to Whole Foods', I think. Something about inspiring and nurturing." Joe was listening intently now, knowing that Heather had disparaged Raina's place of employment in the past.

Heather was looking out the window. "I have to say, I think they take it to heart. At least from what I know."

"Sounds like a good brand," Joe ventured.

"Well, you know Howard Schultz, Starbucks' CEO?" Heather asked. It was a rhetorical question; she plunged ahead. "In 2008, while New Orleans was rebuilding after Hurricane Katrina? He took 10,000 store managers there for an off-site, and on day one, they all did volunteer work."

"Really?" This was news to Joe, even though he bought a Venti Cappuccino at his corner Starbucks at least three times a week. He remembered telling clients over the years about the importance of leading by example. *Howard Schultz apparently gets it*, he thought.

"Yeah, really," Heather continued. "Talk about inspiring and nurturing, right? And knowing that about them made me sort of want to buy their coffee – or at least defend them against friends of mine who think they're driving out smaller neighborhood coffee shops."

Joe changed lanes to make sure he was well-positioned to take the onramp toward his house. He couldn't resist teasing his daughter just a little bit, remembering how, as a teenager, she'd been adamant about having the best of everything. "You're so conscientious all of a sudden," he said, flicking on his turn signal. "I remember a time when you always had to have the brand-name version, no matter what it was! If Starbucks had been around then, I bet you would have spent $50 a week. Minimum."

Heather rolled her eyes at him, but this time it was clear that she was sharing his joke about her teenaged self. "Are we going to do this again, without an audience?" she asked. "Your favorite tease – about you being so focused on making money while we were so into spending it?"

Her use of the word "we" pained Joe a little bit. If he were forced to concede any regrets, they might have to do with not spending more time with his family while the children were growing up. He'd been a classic Boomer Dad in that respect, putting work first while his wife grew bored and his children regarded him more as a chauffeur or a wallet than a parent. *Where are these thoughts coming from?* he wondered. *Does the prospect of retirement just stir this stuff up for everybody?*

"It's kind of about why," he muttered. "Why a person does things. Why they invest any effort in their job. Or, in say, Starbucks' case, why they sell coffee."

"Is that part of your speech?" Heather asked after a moment.

Joe snapped back to the original purpose of the conversation. Now was certainly not the time to be gloomy about retirement or to second-guess his career. On the balance, he was proud of what he had achieved. But still, the question of *why* nagged at him. Maybe it was worth pursuing.

"It could be," Joe said. A funny remembrance came to him, one he thought Heather might appreciate. "You know, in one of the last hiring interviews I did for Ripen. The kid was actually asking ME questions. 'What's your carbon footprint,' he wanted to know. Like, if it wasn't small enough, he wouldn't condescend to work there."

Heather jumped right in, and clearly wasn't taking this as a joke. "Yeah, Dad. That stuff is *important*. Me and all of my friends from college? We've always been focused on the "why" you just mentioned." She seemed to be gaining some steam. "Why do you think Stephen switched his major to environmental law?" she asked, referring to her older brother. Joe was listening, but also admiring her enthusiasm. *I bet she can really drive a boardroom*, he thought.

"It's not just our generation," Heather said, throwing Joe for a loop momentarily. "What about your generation? Why do you think you and Ripen's leadership made the whole Habitat for Humanity thing happen in the past three years?"

Joe had found himself to be a natural internal spokesperson at his last job at Ripen. He had convinced all of the senior management team to donate a week of their own, and their direct reports' time to help build homes for underprivileged families. Politics hadn't really entered into the discussion. It seemed that a lot of Joe's peers were as happy as he was to have the opportunity to swing a hammer. It didn't hurt that one of the most junior staff at Ripen had photographed and blogged the whole thing, down to the last blister. Her YouTube video of the company's involvement had managed to make work with Habitat for Humanity a badge of honor, and

Joe was sure that it was something that was regularly talked up with new recruits.

"Well, Ripen was already an 'organization with a conscience,' right?" Joe said. He meant to downplay his role in the company's involvement with Habitat for Humanity, but his pride in this part of his most recent professional role was evident to his daughter.

"And if I recall, Habitat's CEO approached you first," Heather said, teasingly. "I'm starting to think that they see 'Boomers-who-want-to-give-back' as their new target market."

Joe remembered how engaged and energized Ripen's leadership always seemed to be following these retreats. *Come to think of it, some of our best ideas came in the weeks after we returned to the office*, he thought.

They were nearing the celebration at Joe's house. He'd only lived there for a little more than two years; after the divorce, he'd been the one to move out. The breakup had been fairly amicable, but still, it was odd to think of Donna and Eric still living at the old house, and of Donna's new husband being the one mowing the lawn. But Joe's new neighbors were all very friendly. Most were in their late fifties, and some had already retired themselves. Joe was particularly excited to have met John Loughlin, who was the general manager of the Rattlers, the local National Football League team. Despite his somewhat glamorous job, John was about as down-to-earth as you could get, and a fellow golfer to boot!

Joe was particularly glad that he'd made friends in his new community because the past five years had been pretty rough. There was the separation from Donna, but there was also the challenge of starting a new job when ThinkSmart had been required to downsize its executive team. That stung, but as he'd told Heather, there was a certain justice to it. The experience had been both humbling and eye-opening.

There was a soft glow emitting from the large bay window as he turned into the cul-de-sac. There were already several cars parked on the street, and inside he could see his guests mingling and beginning to enjoy the food, which he was sure was going to be stellar. When his friends insisted on throwing Joe a retirement party, it was his idea to have it at his place, wanting to keep things small and intimate. Donna's old friend Barbara Arruda had agreed to cater the party, and she was a fantastic chef.

For some reason, Joe didn't feel quite ready to go in yet. It would be good to see everyone, of course, but he knew that when he walked through the door, there would be a finality to his retirement that he hadn't fully absorbed.

Heather seemed to understand. She made no move to get out of the car when Joe parked. Sitting with her hands folded in her lap, she picked up the thread of their earlier conversation. "You know," she said, "I feel really lucky to work at a place where I fully support the mission. Even when things get busy or crazy, it seems like everyone there really gets why they're there. Maybe if some of those companies like Enron or whatever had focused more on the *why*, they wouldn't have gone down in history as the poster children for lack of conscience."

"A lot of places learned tough lessons recently," Joe said. "Did you hear that Goldman Sachs recently instituted a policy where their executives are required to donate part of their bonuses to charity?"

"That's encouraging," Heather said. A mischievous twinkle appeared in her eyes. "Hey, I can hardly believe you're into all of this corporate social responsibility stuff. I remember when your favorite movie was "Wall Street." You know, 'greed is good,' etc."

Joe grinned. "Well, I also remember that your mom had such a giant crush on Michael Douglas that she'd watch the movie with me over and over again."

It was a longstanding joke between them that Heather didn't mind finishing for him. "And how life comes full circle, with you now having a giant crush on Michael Douglas's wife!" Two more cars pulled up. It was funny, being sort of a fly on the wall in the BMW, watching old friends and colleagues arrive. And there was something very cozy about sitting in the warm car with Heather, and appreciating that she'd grown into a person that he not only loved, but liked and respected, too.

In front of them, a tall, stooped person unfolded himself from a tiny car with a Zipcar logo. At first, Joe didn't know who the man was at all, and thought he must be the husband or date of one of the other guests. Then he visualized him about fifty pounds heavier, and recognition sank in.

"Holy smokes," he said. "That's Henry Cunningham! Nicest guy I ever met, but maybe the worst manager. I haven't seen him in years."

Engagement

Heather had her hand on the BMW's door handle. She was looking at her father questioningly; on seeing Henry, Joe had relaxed into his seat and was watching as the thinner version of the man he used to know approached Joe's house and was received by the caterer, Barbara Arruda.

"Nicest guy I ever met," Joe found himself saying again. Was it a curse of growing older that you sometimes spoke your thoughts out loud? Or was it the result of years of being a management consultant?

Heather loosened her grip on the door handle with a sigh of impatience that she immediately seemed to feel guilty about. She found a position in the car seat facing Joe. "I thought he was the manager of that division that got shut down at ThinkSmart. The one you kept complaining about over dinner when I was, like, ten." It was sort of endearing, Joe thought, how she couldn't quite eradicate these generational quirks (*Like, you know, whatever. Seriously? Really? Ya think?*) from her speech, even when she was trying to be serious. Or perhaps she did manage it at work, but relaxed into "family mode" around him.

"He was a great guy," Joe said. "But…" he paused for a moment, trying to put his complaint into words. "He thought being a manager was about 'satisfying' his employees. He'd bend over backwards for anybody. And there wasn't any accountability."

"Suddenly I'm ten years old again," Heather said. But she was clearly still listening.

"Hey, consider this your cab fare," Joe retorted. "You said it would be okay if I rehearsed my speech on you. Well, I'm still figuring it out."

To his relief, Heather smiled and nodded at him to continue. Joe sensed that perhaps the feelings of nostalgia that had been nagging him about his retirement might have had similar echoes for her. He tried to see himself through her eyes, and thanked his lucky stars that at least he was still fit and mentally together (and hopefully, not too much of an embarrassment).

"Earlier in my career," he said, "I wish I'd known what I know now. Employees more or less fall into two categories – the ones looking to give, and the ones looking to get. Henry never quite got that 'employee satisfaction' scores didn't mean squat if the division wasn't performing. He had a sort of naïve idea that everyone should be recognized and rewarded in the exact same way, across the board, because that was his idea of fairness. I don't remember a year, actually, in which anybody got a different bonus amount – although of course we weren't supposed to know about that."

Heather was looking at him a bit skeptically. "Why's that so bad?" she asked. "I've got friends that work for Sprout, the internet search engine, and just last month everyone got a $1000 bonus and 10% raise, just because the company was doing well. If they want to spread it around equally, what's wrong with that? It reinforces that everybody's part of the same team. Doesn't that help with 'employee engagement,' or whatever it's called?"

Sprout's decision had been all over the news, with slick and skillfully placed YouTube spots featuring undoubtedly satisfied recipients of the bonus and raise. It helped that Sprout was one of the top "hottest" employers – a name with instant resumé cachet, not to mention some of the swankiest and most forward-thinking job perks around, including free food, pool and ping pong tables, a beer cart on Fridays, and many other "satisfiers." Still, Joe thought the unilateral reward move had been misguided.

"If you're trying to create a sustainable culture," he said, formulating his thoughts as he plowed ahead, "it... well, it can't be done by just handing out carrots." Seeing the look on Heather's face, he changed his tack. "Think about it this way," he said. "What if you and some woman named, I don't know, let's say Jill, were working on the same project. You're logging the same number of hours during the work week, but you know that you're doing the lion's share of the work, including giving up some weekends. In addition, more of your ideas are getting implemented, or incorporated into the final product." He paused, waiting for Heather to imagine the scenario. "What do you think would be the outcome if your boss presented you and Jill with the exact same raise and bonus?"

A vertical line appeared between Heather's eyebrows. "I... I think I'd be mad," she said.

"And what do you think Jill's reaction would be?" Joe asked.

Heather had already tilted her head back, absorbing the point he was making. "I get what you're saying. I'd be thinking, awesome. I'm doing fine. No need to step up my game."

"Exactly," Joe said. He felt a surge of triumph that wasn't unlike what he'd known in his professional capacity, when a CEO or an executive committee had finally seemed to come on board with a plan he was proposing. "Any organization that gives everyone the same bonus or raise regardless of their performance is not only discouraging high performers from continuing to perform – they're discouraging low performers from improving."

Heather looked at him with an expression he interpreted as guarded acceptance. But she wasn't finished playing Devil's Advocate.

"You might be right," she admitted. "But if Sprout's idea of spreading all that money around was so wrong, why does everyone I know still want to work there?"

This seemed like a no-brainer to Joe, and he couldn't resist the opportunity to tease Heather a little bit about the almost legendary perks of Sprout employment. "Because of the indoor swimming pools and gourmet meals, maybe? Or maybe it's the on-the-job massages. I can't keep track."

Heather grinned, and he could see that she was virtually conceding. He would have loved to say something along the lines of, "Vegan quiche and aromatic oils do not a company sustain," but knew she'd just look at him as if he were crazy. "If you make money or perks your differentiator," he said instead, "competitors can easily beat you by just offering more money or better perks."

"Dad," Heather interjected, "We all need to make money. And I'm sure not going to say no to a free on-the-job massage!"

"But money or perks don't motivate long-term," Joe rejoined. "And you just agreed that unfairness is bad for members of pretty much any team, because people care about fairness. Think about your own job," he said, seeing that she was growing impatient. His voice softened. "You don't do it for the money, do you?"

In profile, Heather's face was remarkably like her mother's. But Joe could see himself in the quirk of an eyebrow when she turned toward him again. "That's true," Heather said. "But at the same time, they pay fairly for what I do. It's not like anyone else in my field is making a lot more than me."

Joe smiled. "There's that fairness thing again. And that was Henry's problem." The now-thin figure of Joe's former co-worker had long since been granted entry to the party. "What he didn't realize that while he was trying to make us all happy by rewarding everyone equally, those of us who were really shouldering the burden were getting bitter. Those were the dinner-table conversations you remember," he said. "The ones where I was complaining about Henry even though he was such a nice guy. I was really bothered that he didn't seem to see the difference between what I was contributing and what three or four of my coworkers *weren't*. In trying to be fair to everyone, he wasn't really being fair to anybody. So I jumped on the opportunity to transfer."

Two more cars pulled into the cul-de-sac and passed Joe and Heather, looking for parking. "It's getting crowded, Dad," Heather said quietly. "It's your party and everyone's waiting.

We should go in."

At last, punctuality kicks in, Joe thought. He smiled at Heather, suppressing the urge to ruffle her very grown-up hairdo, and got out of the car.

The entryway was almost alien to him with its tastefully soft lighting. He made a mental note to thank Barbara, the caterer, for her attention to ambience as well as food. Inside, the hustle and bustle of the gathering was already well underway, aided by some wine and beer. Before Heather managed to fade away into the growing crowd, Joe introduced her to some people with what he thought was appropriate fatherly pride. Throughout his entrance to the party, he caught snippets of conversation. Some were about recent developments in popular television shows; some about politics. But a lot seemed to be about work – it seems that given the invitees, that was inevitable. "The true test of a manager is that mutual commitment," Joe overheard. This was from a woman he'd never met who was chatting up Rajesh, who until recently had been Joe's direct report. "You know, where employees are committed to building the company and the company is committed to building the employees. That's the magic formula, and how you engage your employees," the woman continued.

Joe caught Rajesh's eye and they nodded in greeting. *Everyone's got it right in theory,* Joe thought. *Hang in there, Rajesh.* He wondered if the unfamiliar woman might be a new Ripen executive. If so, he hoped she would practice what she preached.

He'd geared himself up for this event and was happy to make the rounds, shaking hands and exchanging hugs where appropriate, always apologizing for being late and blaming it on his daughter, while using even that as an opportunity to boast about her recent accomplishments. The turnout was even better than Joe had expected – he made a mental note to send a substantial thank-you of some sort to his former executive assistant, Lisa, and the rest of the support staff at Ripen. They'd really gone the extra mile in rounding up his past contacts and getting the word out.

Feeling very much the king of his castle, Joe fell in line for some food. As he would have expected, the spread looked amazing. Skewered meats and vegetables were cooking over a portable gas grill, and appetizers of all varieties were making the rounds. At the head of the table, he could see a gorgeously iced cake surrounded by scattered *petits fours*, looking like pink and yellow dice that had just rolled a winning number.

"Hello, Joe," said a husky voice behind him as he reached in to spear some pulled pork. He glanced over his shoulder and almost did a double-take. The person addressing him was Susan Delacourt, whom he still counted as one of his scariest-ever bosses at ThinkSmart.

"Susan!" Joe exclaimed, wiping the serving fork on the edge of his plate. "I don't quite know what to say. I'm delighted to see you. But I must confess… um, I'm a little surprised!"

"I'd never have missed it," Susan said. Her dark, curly hair had a more pronounced streak of white in the front than it had when Joe had worked with her. She looked older, and to Joe's eye, maybe even more commanding than he remembered. Despite being a good foot shorter than him, she had somehow always been able to seem like the tallest person in the room.

He had to conceal his surprise when she continued, "You were always one of my favorites."

"I-I was? Really?" Joe smiled at the tone of his own voice; it was as if the captain of the cheerleaders in high school had suddenly condescended to sit next to him at lunch.

"You're surprised to see me," Susan said. She was looking at him from under those same heavy lids, and with that same assessing air, that he once knew to dread. But she was smiling, all the same.

Joe shuffled forward in the line at the table and reached for one of the four salads on offer – candied walnuts and pears in some creamy dressing looked good. "A bit, actually," he said. "I mean… we never really got to know each other personally, did we? You were one of the most respected managers at ThinkSmart, but… don't take this the wrong way, you were also one of the most distant. I don't know, maybe I was intimidated by you."

Susan's smile broadened. She reached for the same salad Joe had selected. "Well, I always tried to keep something of a separation between myself and the employees I was leading," she said. "At the time, it was pretty necessary. 95 percent of our management team were men! I had to make sure I didn't seem too soft. Or worse, too motherly."

Joe had never considered Susan's standoffishness as a tactic in what had been, as she said, a pretty male-dominated workplace. She'd been referred to as something of a shrew, actually, during the after-work cocktail hours she'd never attended. But her results could never have been argued.

"To be honest, Susan, you might not have been my favorite manager," Joe blurted out. "It sounds a bit awful to say, put that way. But you did make my life tough at times."

"I hope so," Susan said. She seemed to be taking the conversation in the vein Joe meant it – as lighthearted reflection. "If you recall, our division was always first."

That was true. And to be fair, Joe had to admit he had learned a lot under Susan's auspices, even if it had seemed like a hard slog at the time. "You held me accountable," he said. "I remember dreading having to justify my numbers. It was kind of a running joke, you know?" he says, alluding to those after-hours complaints. "*Look out for Susan and her spreadsheets.* But you were always respectful," he pointed out. "And you know, over time I think I respected you more and more."

Susan's smile had settled in. Now that so many years had passed, Joe wondered why he'd never before seen her extraordinary resemblance to a housecat: small and round, but with such sharp eyes, not to mention the claws she held in reserve. "And no one ever seemed to leave under your watch," he added. "I mean, sure, there were transfers and promotions. But people in your division tended to stick around."

"You were one of the better ones," Susan said simply. "As I think you'll recall, I had – I have, still – zero tolerance for mediocrity. And in my experience, high-performing employees seek out other high-performers. So I ended up with a pretty sleek and effective team, and together we earned a reputation for high performance. That's not something you walk away from, generally, especially if you've helped build it."

Joe accepted a glass of Malbec from the bartender. "I guess the proof of the pudding is that you're still there, at ThinkSmart," he said. "In other words, you survived the cuts." He found himself very interested in what Susan had to say. A quick survey of the party revealed it to be well in hand; perhaps he could afford some one-on-one time. "Listen, would you like to sit for a minute?" he asked. "It looks like we could squeeze in over there –" he gestured at the couch – "if one of us takes the ottoman."

"Happy to," Susan said. "It's been a busy week. Nights like these, I envy you, going into retirement. I suppose I haven't said 'Congratulations,' yet?"

Joe laughed. "No. But that was never your style, was it?"

Susan settled into the couch and Joe took the ottoman (*Boy, some things never change,* he thought). She placed her wine glass on the side table, balancing her plate on her knees. She took a bite of a mushroom-and-caramelized-onion tartlet, looking more like a housecat than ever. It was hard, in this moment, to remember her as the tiger at the head of the meeting room, calling everyone to task for their metrics.

"One of the things I remember most about you is those monthly all-hands meetings," Joe said. "You'd cover the company's overall performance, our region's performance, and our office's performance. And then you'd meet with each of us one-on-one to explain how our own individual performance was contributing. Boom, boom, boom," he said. Susan was nodding. Her expression was an oddly familiar one: as a boss, she'd had a way of tightening her lips that meant something along the lines of, *Okay buddy, get to the point.* "I never knew why you went to such effort to share those details with us," Joe said.

"One of the things I learned early on," Susan said, "was the importance of alignment. I know a lot of you guys might have found those meetings tedious. But it was important for you to know how the whole company was doing. I had to make sure I was setting your goals so that they were aligned with the business. See, having you understand how the business was doing, and how your work was contributing, was my way of creating 'line of sight.' Over the years, I've found that is essential in engaging employees in the business."

"It must have worked," Joe said. "For seven years running, we were the top-performing division. Heck," he added, "if we could have hired more quickly, maybe we could have done even better than that!" He stuffed a bite of that pear and candied-nut salad into his mouth and was immediately convinced that Barbara had outdone herself. He hadn't realized how hungry he'd gotten.

"There was a reason for that too, Joe," Susan said. "If you'll indulge me, I'll bring up that adage that I'm sure you guys got tired of hearing when you worked for me. 'Hire hard, live easy; hire easy, live hard.' I was pretty diligent about hiring for the behaviors and traits that would perform best for us." Joe laughed, replying "And don't forget your favorite acronym – B.E.S.T. Education and Skills are important…"

Here Susan chimed in, nodding, and they finished the axiom in unison. "…but Behaviors and Traits are the difference between mediocrity and high performance."

"I think you brought that up every time we hired someone," Joe said. "Obviously, I committed it to memory!"

Joe had always been famous for the quick doodles he used to illustrate his thoughts, and was much more comfortable, in fact, sketching on a paper napkin over drinks than laboriously making PowerPoint graphics. He could easily have drawn Susan's B.E.S.T. chart from memory:

BEHAVIOR	EDUCATION	SKILLS	TRAITS
How one acts or reacts to specific circumstances	The information a person carries with him or herself	The ability to put information into action	Characteristics that define one's personal nature

"You certainly had good instincts that way." He remembered some of Susan's hires that had seemed odd at the time – when she opted for one or two team members whose resumes didn't seem as fully developed, or whose credentials seemed a little left-of-field. But following her B.E.S.T. principles, somehow she'd managed not to make many bad calls.

"You know what I said a few minutes ago, about high performers being drawn to other high performers?" Susan said, leaning forward. Her long necklace brushed her salad. "Shoot. Now I have dressing on this." While wiping the beads off, she continued, "To encourage high performance, you have to hire other high performers. And it's not easy to hire high performers, unfortunately."

What she said made sense to Joe, although he'd become used to the more usual way of doing things: hiring the person with the best degrees, depth of experience, and appropriate skills, even if they might not seem like the best fit for the team based on the things that motivated them and kept them engaged. With chagrin, he realized that he'd probably seen more turnover among people he'd hired in the last five years than Susan had seen over her entire career.

A familiar face broke him out of his introspection. "Bob!" he called. He stood up, placing his picked-at plate on the ottoman and waving a hand. "Bob!"

Bob Brustlin saw Joe and gave him a nod. He finished the conversation he'd been having and came over to Susan and Joe.

"Susan, let me introduce you to Bob Brustlin," Joe said. "He's the CEO of VHB, the engineering company. Bob, this is Susan Delacourt of ThinkSmart. She's just been letting me know how much better they're getting on without me." Joe winked at Susan and continued his introduction. "Bob has been one of my favorite clients recently," he said. "A few minutes ago, Susan was telling me about alignment. If I recall correctly, one of your differentiators was that your employees were always aligned, have I got that right?"

Bob Brustlin was one of those unassuming people whose voices tended to carry all the more because it was quiet and precise. "I was always a fan of establishing a communication promise," he said. "We commit to our employees by telling them, 'This is what we will communicate, this is when we'll communicate it, this is who we'll communicate it to, and here is why.' And so you formalize it. At VHB, we actually post our communication promise in all of our conference rooms. That way, you're reinforcing alignment up and down throughout the organization."

Susan offered Bob a warm smile and turned back to Joe. It was a relief to see the humor flickering behind those gray-green eyes Joe had once viewed as so obstinate. "Suddenly, those old meetings make more sense, eh, Joe?"

Susan and Bob seemed absorbed in the conversation that followed. Joe managed to quiet his growling stomach with the rest of the salad, a few tartlets, and a hearty serving of pulled pork. He sipped his wine, listening to Susan and Bob getting to know one another, but aware that as the ostensible guest of honor, he ought to get back into the fray. He scanned the crowd – it really was a crowd now. People were packed into every square foot of floor space. He glimpsed Heather in a corner, talking earnestly with a young man he recognized as the son of a Ripen colleague. *Good for her*, he thought.

He recognized another familiar face. "Chris!" he called. The woman didn't hear him, but Joe was confident he could get her attention soon. "Excuse me, but I see Christine Schuster over there; have you met? She did an amazing job of improving the performance at Emerson Hospital during a really difficult time in the healthcare industry. "Chris!" Joe called again. Unfortunately, her attention had just been engaged by another partygoer. But Joe's gestures in her direction had attracted the attention of the man she'd been conversing with. He was of medium height, with fair hair cropped close to his head and what seemed like a congenitally sardonic expression. He met Joe's glance and to Joe's shock, nodded and came towards him.

It was Ed Burns, a person Joe had never expected to see again. That is, since he'd fired him two years ago.

High Performance

Joe remembered it as if it was yesterday, and still with some discomfort. It was never easy to let someone go, but he'd had a sinking feeling that was what was in store when he'd summoned Ed to his office at Ripen for what would be their third conversation about Ed's underperformance. With dark, mocking eyes and a reputation for arrogance, not to mention talking over others at meetings, Ed seemed to think that he knew better than any of his coworkers – but in particular, better than Joe. It was difficult to feel that any message was really getting across, and the less pleasant the message, the more defensive or sarcastic Ed was likely to be.

"Please close the door and have a seat," Joe had said. Ed had stalked into his office a few minutes early and was standing with his arms crossed. *Great*, Joe remembered thinking. *His body language is already saying that he's not going to listen.*

Ed sat, his arms still folded across his chest. "Is this going to take long?" he asked. "I've got a presentation to prepare for Northwestern Global." Ed was justly famous around the office for his meticulous client presentations, but he was also notorious for guarding them zealously. Heaven forbid that anyone suggest he ask for anyone else's input or assistance. He almost seemed to relish working long hours on occasion, and never shied away from expressing the opinion that anybody else "would just screw it up."

"This meeting isn't going to be easy for you or for me," Joe said, deciding to cut to the chase without leaving Ed many opportunities for remarks that would make things even more difficult. "As you know, we've already had some conversations about your attitude and your unwillingness to be a team player with some of our other divisions."

Ed interrupted. "I know what my numbers are. So do you! I'm in the top 20% of producers. So I think your perception of my 'attitude' isn't really that relevant."

Boy, case in point, thought Joe. "It isn't just me," he had replied. It's many of your colleagues as well. People don't want to work with you, and you continually make it clear that you prefer not to work with other people."

"Like how?" Ed asked. "Yeah, I have high standards and I don't mind who knows it. Half the time it's faster to just do everything myself instead of having to go back and take care of other people's mistakes."

"I've already given you countless examples," Joe interrupted , determined to retain the upper hand and stick to the facts. "Just this past week, for instance. Even though you know that Barry in Cincinnati is our resident expert on audit protocols, you talked over him in the client meeting and positioned yourself as the expert. That was a pretty remarkable decision on your part," Joe continued, "considering that even you would have to agree that auditing isn't your strong suit."

"Hey, look," Ed said. "Barry has some talent. But he's only been here nine months! He hasn't earned his stripes yet, and for God's sake, he looks like a kid. What is he, 30?"

"This isn't about your opinion, Ed," Joe retorted, "and the decisions that get made around here aren't based on tenure or a person's age. They're based on capability. You already know what the outcome was – the client has now gone out to bid, even though Ripen has worked with them for two years."

Ed looked unfazed. "Well, I'm going to say that that's their loss. Look, it's not like they're a big earner for us, or even a consistent one. I would think that my track record with our clients would speak pretty amply in my favor."

"Losing the job wasn't the only result," Joe said. "Or even the most important one. I've now had Barry approach me to say that he doesn't want to work with you again. That's just flat-out disruptive."

"I'd call it flat-out immature," Ed said, staring Joe down. "What are we, in kindergarten here?"

"We're in business, here, Ed," Joe said. "The sustainability of our product is what's at issue. And you don't seem to be able to accept the fact that your attitude is counterproductive or to rein it in, even though you've been given several opportunities.

"Look," Joe continued, sketching a simple four-quadrant diagram on his notepad. Even though he'd shown it to Ed before, he wanted to be sure that the direct report understood the full brunt of the trouble he was in.

In the diagram's four boxes, Joe jotted **Transition,
Decision Time, Potential,** and **Star.** On its axes, he wrote
PERFORMANCE and **VALUES.** "I know you think you're
here–" he said, pointing to the **Star** box. Ed sighed as if Joe
were wasting his valuable time. He seemed to be making a
conscious effort not to glance at the clock on the office wall.
"But the fact of the matter is that your attitude has put you
into this category," Joe said sharply, indicating **Decision Time.**
"And the only progress you seem to be making lately is going
to take you right out the door."

This was true. Previous conversations of this type had
not yielded any results, and it had often been within a matter of
hours that Ed was taking out his frustrations on his coworkers.

For every snide comment that he managed to withhold for fear of losing his job, there was a tirade waiting for the next person who caught him in the wrong mood. And his moods, in Joe's estimation, were pretty much never "right" for the organization.

"I can't believe I'm being called on the carpet for just asserting my authority in a damn meeting," Ed said with exasperation, as if determined to dig himself even deeper. "And I can't believe that some kid, whose numbers aren't even half mine, is whining to you. And that you're taking his side!"

Joe felt a twinge of unexpected sympathy – partly because in his heart of hearts he knew what was going to happen. *I'm going to have to bring in HR to begin a formal corrective action plan*, he thought. *And from there it's pretty inevitable that Ed is out of here.* It was a shame; on occasion, it was clear that Ed could be a decent guy. He did have the talent; it was that ego that had to go. *At least, if and when it happens, he'll get good severance*, Joe thought. *Ripen understands the importance of treating people the right way – even people being released. If this had been ThinkSmart, they would have probably just escorted him to the door three months ago and made a permanent enemy of him.* At least Ripen seemed to know, as Joe himself believed, that sometimes a person was just a bad fit. He respected the company for their policy of fairness and generosity when letting someone go, because he knew that it was better if ex-employees spoke well of Ripen. In addition to knowing that they could become future clients, or even join up with a company that acquired Ripen, Joe also understand that a disgruntled employee could really tarnish a company's reputation if they were diligent about voicing their discontent.

"Stuff's changing, Ed," Joe had said in a measured tone. "These 'kids,' as you term them, have got a lot to offer that somehow you're not seeing. You're going to have to learn to accept them better than you've been doing and to treat them as peers. That means not just in front of clients, but in regular staff meetings. And that means consistently."

Ed snorted and pushed his chair back. "Are we done here? I need to get back to making Ripen some money."

Wow, he still doesn't get it, Joe thought. "We're done with this meeting, yes," he said, and watched, bemused, as Ed stalked out of his office.

The man coming toward Joe now, at the party, hadn't lost his stiff way of walking or even his permanently sardonic expression, but Joe was surprised to see that there was a smile on his face. Ed walked up to Joe and held out a hand. Joe had to restrain himself from looking to make sure there wasn't a dead rat in it, or something of that sort.

"Congratulations," Ed said, meeting Joe's startled look with a firm handshake and a smile of sincere pleasure. "It's the beginning of a well-deserved retirement for you."

"Thanks for coming," Joe said. "I've got to tell you, this party's been full of surprises so far. But given the circumstances of our last meeting, you're one of the last people I'd have expected to be here."

"I've been meaning to talk to you about that," Ed said. "Almost put it in an email, actually. But then I heard from Karen that you were having some folks over tonight, so I figured I'd drop by. Hope you don't mind. We're actually neighbors – I'm right around the corner on Clement Street."

"Of course not," Joe said, still a bit mystified. "But listen… about Ripen. I hope you know that I wasn't in a position to give many people much of a leash if things weren't working."

Ed was shaking his head. "You know that email I was going to write you? Believe it or not, it was to say 'thank you.' So… thank you."

High Performance

"Thank you?" Joe scoured Ed's face for a trace of sarcasm, hardly able to believe what he was hearing.

"That's right," Ed said. "I mean that, sincerely. You actually gave me one of the best business lessons I've ever received."

Joe couldn't suppress a laugh. "You'll have to forgive me if I say I never would have known it at the time. You never seemed eager to accept a lesson from anyone, least of all me."

"I'd gotten complacent," Ed admitted. "I'd become satisfied that my performance was up to anyone's standards, so I wasn't worried that my attitude was a problem, even when you pointed it out to me. Truth be told, I was pretty unhappy a lot of the time at Ripen and I got into a habit of taking it out on everybody else."

Joe couldn't deny that that had been the case. "You were always a performer," he said instead. "But during that window of time, we also needed team players. It's funny, I was just talking to Susan Delacourt about alignment. And at Ripen we needed people who could work together and who shared the company's goals and struggles. I think one of the things I was trying to get through to you was that it wasn't just what you did, but how and why you did it."

51

"You were fair with me," Ed said. "We had numerous conversations where you encouraged me to improve my attitude and get on board. But in case you don't recall, I've never been great at taking criticism." He winked. "Believe it or not, I also appreciated how you handled things, Joe. It took me a while to admit it to myself, but I know you could have terminated me 'for cause' if you'd wanted to. So I appreciated your calling it a 'layoff,' and making it seem like just part of the company restructuring. That allowed me to save face, and helped me explain why I was no longer at Ripen when I started interviewing again. So I was going to thank you for that in the email as well."

What a change, Joe thought. The man conversing with him now was so very different from the sullen, arrogant person who'd made life hell for so many people at Ripen. "I'm touched that you're here," Joe said. "And I really appreciate what you're saying. It's nice to know that you don't have any hard feelings – I guess that means I did something right."

"Well, I can't say I really appreciated it at the time," Ed admitted. "Things were pretty rough for a little while there. I thought I'd have a ton of other job offers. And it was pretty humbling to have to look for a job for twelve months."

Joe winced. "Yeah, don't worry about it," Ed continued. You gave me a wake-up call. My attitude really did need to change. I was rolling into all of these job interviews convinced that I'd just blow them out of the water, and I didn't realize that if they had the option to hire me or someone who wasn't so convinced he was the hot commodity, they might go for the second option."

Joe nodded. "But you did find another position, even if it took some time?" he asked.

Ed grinned. "Yeah. Well, I did have to take a lower-level, lower-paying job. But here's the weird thing – I'm working as hard as ever, but I'm actually enjoying it more. At Ripen, I was really just taking things one day at a time. I'd get bitter about staying late at the office or even about just coming in. The slightest setback would just get me so angry. Recently, I read something about 'disengagement,' and the definition seemed to fit me – I was disengaged in my job. I didn't like the clients much, and I didn't really care for the work itself. Well, except for the presentations," he admitted. "I confess I did get a kick out of winning the work."

"That much was pretty obvious," Joe said. "But you've just made a pretty important distinction – there's a real difference between being motivated just for one day or one client, and being motivated in the job itself."

"I know that now," Ed said. "Now, I'm working with clients I really respect, in a job I really like. And the whole direction of the firm – I can get behind it. It's a bit less money, but I'm a lot happier about earning it."

"Makes all the difference," Joe said. He smiled to himself, thinking briefly of another drawing he'd tried to show Ed back when he'd thought there was a chance the younger man's performance might improve. A simple Venn diagram, it depicted three circles labeled **what I like to do**, **what I'm good at**, and **what needs to get done**.

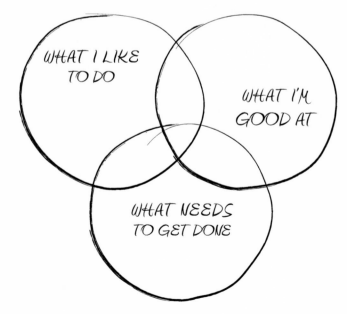

It seemed that perhaps Ed had at last figured out a way to balance those three critical elements. Joe always felt that the more these three circles overlapped, the greater the chance of an employee reaching high performance *and* being engaged.

He could see a few people at the other end of the room conferring and glancing in his direction. Barbara's staff was setting out coffee and brandy, and appeared nearly ready to cut the cake. "I suppose I ought to mingle," he said to Ed. "It's good to see you. I hope you enjoy yourself tonight. Thanks again for coming. And thanks for the thanks."

"Hear, hear," Ed said, tipping his beer. As if on cue, the group of people Joe had been about to head toward raised their glasses and the air was filled with the tinkle of silverware on stemware and calls of "Speech! Speech!"

Here we go, Joe thought. *I sure hope I do this right. Who knows when I'll get another opportunity?* He looked around for Heather; she was talking to an older couple. He caught her eye and she smiled encouragingly as he made his way toward the catering table and the gathering circle of friends and colleagues.

Innovation

Although he was an experienced public speaker, Joe was still prone to a few butterflies. In this case, he experienced more than a few – partly because he hadn't fully formulated his thoughts, and partly because this was unlike presenting to an executive team as a consultant. This was *personal*. He was also aware of the need to not drone on and on in a disorganized fashion; it was a party, after all.

The smiling people surrounding him, many of whom were already raising their glasses in a silent toast, put him at his ease. Remembering a Toastmasters best practice, he sought out the friendliest face in the crowd: Heather, who gave him a reassuring nod. She was standing next to Deb Allen, a client with whom Joe had once butted heads. He'd actually been sorry that his advice to Deb, which she neglected to implement, had been proven correct, because he liked her so much. Tall and athletic (Joe remembered that she was an accomplished runner), Deb had a wry sense of humor that Joe had often enjoyed both in meetings and over the occasional lunch or cocktail. With a twinge of guilt, he realized that he'd fallen out of touch with her and had little idea how she was occupying herself these days. He knew that Gametime, the 400-store chain of video game rentals she had headed when Joe had last been her management consultant, had gone bankrupt a few years ago. In its heyday, Gametime had been the number-one profit generator in Deb's sector, a fact of which she'd been justifiably proud.

While preoccupied with these momentary regrets, Joe had an idea of how to frame his address to the group.

He cleared his throat. "Thank you all for coming," he began. "How do these speeches usually start? It probably sounds like a cliché, but I can wholeheartedly say that I'm humbled, proud, and delighted to be here with all of you, although a little sad. I'm way too young to be retiring, of course – feel free to reinforce that throughout the evening, will you?" There were some appreciative laughs from his audience, although not as many as he would have liked to hear. He continued. "I didn't prepare a lot of words, and I want to get back to mingling with you and catching up on old times." At this, he caught Ed Burns indulging in a behavior that was much more amusing than it had been when they worked together – rolling his eyes. But he was clearly doing it for Joe's benefit – there were a few more scattered chuckles.

"I did want to leave you with some thoughts about my career," Joe said. "I suppose that's traditional, too. But in chatting with you tonight, and in seeing so many old colleagues and friends, some of those thoughts have been reinforced. And I hope, developed further. You know, they say an active mind keeps you spry, right?" Ed Burns was positively grinning now.

"Many of you remember one of my favorite business axioms – I know I must have said it a lot, especially in the past several years. In my career, and in my continued opinion, I've learned that business can't be a 100-yard dash, no matter how exciting that seems in the short term. To be sustainable, a business has to be a marathon." Joe knew that this metaphor would resonate with Deb Allen, and although he'd surely said it to her before, she didn't seem to mind hearing it again. "The mistake that a lot of companies make is to focus too exclusively on the present, without creating a model that has ongoing potential. Basically, if you are too focused on short-term profit, you're behaving like the farmer who eats his seeds."

Heather emitted a barely audible sigh; she was pretty used to his occasional overdependence on metaphors. Joe moved on. "I know I've occasionally been guilty of that sort of shortsightedness, not just at work, but with family." Here, he had to swallow to cover a catch in his throat. "But when you're retiring, of course, you're reevaluating the mistakes you've made, as well as the successes. And to me, there appears to be a theme." He paused for effect. "It's the need to continue to change who we are – as people, as businesses, and as leaders. And that… well, it got me thinking that creativity is the cornerstone of life. It keeps us vibrant and engaged, and empowered to think differently."

Always a bit more comfortable with a visual reference, Joe remembered a relevant diagram from one of the many business books he has read over the past couple of years.

"Apparently there's research that bears out my point," he said. "Creativity is at its highest point in childhood, and declines throughout adulthood. So does laughter and question-asking, in fact."

"I bet you wish you had a flipchart right now," Deb Allen called, bringing a tumult of giggles to the floor. Joe's propensity for drawing to illustrate his points was well known. He realized that he could, in fact, see the referenced chart in his mind's eye now:

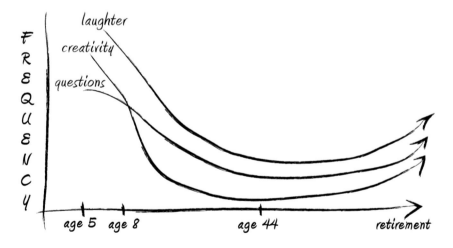

"You know me too well," he responded, looking purposefully sheepish for a brief moment. "But the point of the chart was to depict how all of those things – creativity, laughter, and question-asking – go through a sharp decline until retirement. And in some ways, I liken that to business. I remember that the most fun and most productive days at ThinkSmart were when we were small and quick. When we 'grew up,' so to speak, we got slow and bureaucratic. We had less fun. And instead of continuing to ask really important, open-ended questions like 'Why?' or 'Why not?' we became creatures of 'Because.' *We tried that before but it didn't work because...* or *We can't expand globally because...* or *We can't pursue that new market because...* or *We can't offer flex time because..."*

Joe was really warming to his topic now (and not missing his flipchart as much). He could see heads nodding in agreement, especially among those of his old ThinkSmart colleagues. "So I guess if there's some parting advice I can offer, it's to stay more like children. Or to learn how to be like retirees, maybe." This last was met with more chuckles. "Because, you know, some organizations on a variety of scales are asking the same questions. Southwest Airlines was allowed to ask 'Why.' And they're continuing to change their industry. 'Why not fly into regional airports instead of the more traditional major (and expensive) cities? Why not omit the baggage fees that our competitors are charging?'"

Joe located Henry Cunningham, standing about half a head above the back row of Joe's guests. He gestured toward him. "Henry there took a Zipcar to get here tonight. That's a company that asked 'why.' And just the other day, I was having breakfast with Dr. Allen Marr from Geocomp, who was talking to me about his latest product. Now why is that interesting? Because he's CEO of a *consulting firm* that also *develops products.* Dr. Marr is naturally curious, and always pushes his employees to ask, 'Why not?'"

Susan Delacourt, stepping into a role she'd often fulfilled when she'd been Joe's supervisor, helped him keep his focus now. "So it's not just that business is a marathon, is what you're saying," she said, loudly enough to be heard above any party murmurs. "It's that you have to create your own race."

"Right," Joe said. "And before I let you all get to that wonderful-looking dessert, I'd just like to point out that technology is pretty key to doing what Susan just said: creating your own race. I know that as I've gotten older, I've embraced new technologies slower than I should have. For example, my daughter Heather continues to text me; I continue to leave her voice mail messages that go unanswered." Many of Joe's listeners could apparently relate to this experience with their own children, because they chuckled in appreciation. A few heads turned in Heather's direction, but she was self-possessed enough not to blush. "Technology is changing the entire pace of the world we live in. And if we don't continue to explore and to ask questions, our businesses will end up running in someone else's marathon. And that's usually a hard slog.

"So as you're enjoying your cake and hopefully making some new acquaintances, I'd just encourage you to think about how you can go back to your offices, stores, branches, agencies, schools, or wherever, and challenge the norm. If you're big enough to have company policies, I encourage you to take a look at how they're written. Over the years, I concluded that policies are mostly in place to protect us against the few who might abuse their privileges. But they suffocate creativity and empowerment. Re-write your policies to be guardrails and gateways, not concrete walls and obstacles, to creativity. And don't wait until your own retirement to start asking 'Why' and 'Why not.'

This seemed to be a good stopping point, so he concluded, "Cheers. And thank you again for coming."

Joe didn't think he was flattering himself that the applause that followed his speech was more than polite. It was pretty enthusiastic, in fact, and to his delight he could see that people who had been standing next to one another didn't immediately head for a plate or a refill, but struck up conversations among themselves. Curiously, he felt somewhat deflated. Perhaps it was the knowledge that the opportunity to share thoughts like these would now, in retirement, be few and far between. *But it's more than that,* he thought. *I just made a big deal of the importance of asking "Why." Could it be that I'm only retiring **because** it's the "thing to do" at my age, with my accomplishments?*

As he was making his way through the crowd in something of a reflective haze, shaking hands with well wishers, he noticed that there appeared to be one other person who also appeared lost in thought, despite Joe's expectations that she'd be the first to approach him with a wisecrack or two. Deb's recent experiences at Gametime, which had prompted many of Joe's remarks, had clearly got her thinking about some of their last conversations, when Joe had been trying to push her to invest more resources and technology for the future.

He remembered their long-ago meeting. "Joe," Deb had said, shaking her head and clearly not in a joking mood, "We have tons of pressure on us from shareholders to maximize profits this quarter. Diverting resources and funds to invest in virtual gaming is just not where we're at. Not to mention that some of my team members believe the technology will never evolve to the point where it's a solid revenue stream for anybody – and if even it does, there's no telling whether there'll be profit in it for us."

Joe had been a little surprised at her continued reluctance. In addition to enjoying her confidence and personality, he had respected what she had been able to build after she took over as President and CEO of Gametime. However, he was convinced that she was being shortsighted. "You have to look outside the video gaming industry," he had encouraged her. "Your business is going to fail if you don't keep your eye on the future. People are already playing games on the Internet. And companies like GreenCine and Netflix are figuring out new distribution methods. At a certain point, don't you think people are going to stop coming into your stores?"

"People will always want to see and play the game before they buy it," Deb protested, clearly not budging in what she was convinced was the truth. "Plus, with our rental model, when someone gets tired of a game, they can just come in and exchange it for something else. That low-cost, no-commitment model has been our differentiator from the very beginning."

"And I'm not suggesting that you abandon that model," Joe exhorted. "But I think you have to at least consider diversifying your distribution methods. And you have to start thinking more globally! If you were able to rent virtually in Europe or India or Japan, without the cost of storefronts and on-site staff –"

"That's an investment that I don't think we can make, at least not this year," Deb interjected. "I don't think you quite 'get' the pressure that I and the rest of the board are under to deliver results right now. Shareholders have expectations."

"You need to look out for your customers and employees first," Joe chided. "Many a great company has gone belly-up after satisfying short-term shareholder goals." Because of the ease Joe's banter with Deb usually took, he felt he could afford to be extremely blunt. "Listen. I hate to point it out," he said. "But the average age of your executive team is 55. You don't look like your customers anymore, and the trouble is, you're not thinking like them, either." Deb had the good humor to give him a look of exaggerated dismay and joke, "I'll have you know that I'm only 47 years young, sir."

Joe smiled, but he wasn't quite ready to give up. "As your management consultant, I'm pleading with you to reconsider. Think about the changes we've seen just in the last couple of years. Earlier in my career, I recall Polaroid and Kodak ignoring digital innovation because they were afraid to undermine their flagship products and films. How many people do you know now, aside from maybe a true aficionado with a darkroom, who isn't using a digital camera of some sort? We've seen print newspapers and CD manufacturers decline – you can't argue with me there, either."

"Look," Deb said. "While we're being blunt here… you're not a technical person. I am. I don't think that the manufacturers of the games are going to be expending their own resources to create a model where their customers can just snap their fingers and get whatever they want. That's Star Trek stuff. And as for Netflix… well, I give them five years, tops. Dropping video games in the mail is not going to work for Gametime either, for the same reasons. Shrinkage. Mailing costs. We don't have the resources to be chasing down delinquent discs – and come to think of it, we'd lose our late-fee revenue."

Fortunately, that hadn't been quite the last conversation Joe and Deb had had. But he was again aware of their lapse in communication as he made his way toward her. He'd heard that Gametime had continued to struggle and had eventually gone under, but he hadn't reached out to Deb to express his condolences or offer advice. By that time, he had been laid off from ThinkSmart and was busy trying to develop a new group of clients at Ripen. It wasn't that he hadn't thought about it – but he could admit to himself that he hadn't known quite how to approach her without reminding her that, well, he'd "told her so."

Now, at the retirement party, he found himself drifting toward her. Heather was still standing next to Deb, and the older woman was absorbed in something that Joe's daughter was showing her on Heather's phone. Approaching them from behind, he placed a hand on Deb's arm. "Hey, stranger," he said. "I'm so glad you could make it. It's been way too long."

Deb gave him a rueful smile. "It sure has. I was glad to be included on your guest list. We always worked pretty well together, and… I'm not out of the game just yet. I caught you looking over here during your little lecture. I know you didn't mean to single me out, but obviously, all that talk about building sustainable business models and innovating hit home."

Heather glanced up from her phone. Looking over her shoulder, Joe could see that she was downloading an episode of *Lost*. "Be careful, Deb," Heather joked. "If you keep it up he'll resume his speech! And he'll start off by saying something about how 'the architect of the present can't design the future.' That's one of his favorites."

"She loves to tease me," Joe said. "And I let her, because we both know that if I'd remembered that one while I was talking I'd have figured out a way to fit it in!"

Deb laughed. "Well, it must run in the family, then. Heather was just showing me the million-and-two things she can do on her new phone, and I've been thinking about how much I need to upgrade. And not just my personal technology – I do want to make that clear. I need an upgrade of my ideas, if I'm going to get back in the game. And you know – I have this feeling that I'm not quite done yet. Maybe with enough 'Whys' and 'Why nots,' I'll come up with the next iPod. You know, have some crazy idea and then make the technology get there instead of relying on it to underwrite the idea."

It was clear that she'd been recalling the same conversations as Joe, which made him a little uncomfortable. He was very pleased that his former client and sometime friend was showing a bit of her usual feistiness. And the thought that he could have inspired her in any way was pretty gratifying. But still, he felt the need to lighten the tone a bit. Turning to Heather again, he mock-scolded, "Young lady. Did I catch you texting during my talk?"

Joe and Deb exchanged a glance. Among people their age, a joke about how buried in their devices many younger people were was always at least a tad welcome.

Heather took it in stride, as usual. "Dad, I've told you before that my generation can multitask! Plus, you know I've been hearing that stuff about 'innovating for the future' from you for years – right down to your favorite turns of phrase, as I think I just pointed out."

"I know," Joe said, still teasing. "I was paying attention."

"Well, you should have been here just a couple of minutes ago then to hear Deb picking my brain about technology. I told her she should talk to some of my coworkers' kids. They've grown up using technology; they practically think an iPad is a piece of paper!"

Joe had tinkered with his younger son's iPad and found himself enjoying it immensely, though it was hard to imagine something of that sort ever replacing his beloved doodles and sketches as his first choice in communicating his ideas. He turned back to Deb. "You know, it is virtually impossible to anticipate how things are going to go," he said, gently conceding the fears that had contributed to Gametime's demise. "These kids, I'm sure they will think of ways of using technology that I certainly can't anticipate."

Deb gave him a trademark look of superiority, but Joe beat her to the punch: "But then," he continued with a wink, "that isn't my field."

Tri-Branding

The party wound down as the night wore on. Interacting with so many old friends had Joe keyed up, and that was a familiar feeling. Although he could be focused on any number of tasks during the day, he really came to life around people. One of his few worries about retirement was making time to socialize, and with whom. Even if he had still been married and living with Donna and his youngest son, Eric, Joe suspected he might get a bit cabin-feverish being around the house all day. He'd never been the type to retreat into television or even books for very long stretches of time. His work had truly been a passion; he wasn't looking forward to waking up in his still-new house without a full agenda ahead of him. *Thank goodness for golf,* he found himself thinking as he saw his last guest out the door. *Working on my game ought to keep me occupied until I settle in to having so much more free time.*

"Thanks so much, Barbara," he said to the caterer as she and her staff packaged up the scant leftovers and transferred them to his mostly empty refrigerator. "Everything was absolutely delicious. I think you've probably made some new clients – at least four people asked for your contact information tonight!"

Barbara winked. "I made sure to have extra business cards on hand," she said. "Did you see these? My daughter helped me pick them out." She handed him the remnants of the stack. The cards were very slender – no more than a half-inch in height – and depicted only Barbara's business name, Bon Mot, and logo. Tastefully, yet prominently featured was a QR code. Joe had only just gotten used to seeing them. Most recently, he'd run across several in an art museum he'd visited with Eric the previous month. By scanning the codes in the exhibit with his mobile phone, he was treated to a recording of detailed information about the painter's technique on each particular work. He'd been delighted; Eric, predictably nonplussed. But then, Eric knew all about art already, and had grown up with a mobile phone in his pocket.

"Very nice," he commented, replacing the card in the stack as Barbara folded tablecloths. "I remember when my assistants used to spend hours entering contact information from those things into a database, after conferences."

"I actually did that myself," Barbara said, "although that was in the days of rotary files. I worked as a receptionist while I was putting myself through culinary college. I used to dread when the attorneys would come back from meetings with a bunch of cards I'd have to file. These days, you just point and 'bloop!' There's the information, right there. There's even a free app for it."

"Very handy," Joe agreed, as Heather came back into the room. "Hi, sweetheart. You about ready to go? Would you like to take some of this food home?"

Heather's eyes lit up. Joe knew she didn't have much time or inclination to cook. "Can I?" she asked. "Oooh. That would be awesome. I swear I ate soup for lunch this whole past week. And it wasn't that yummy parsnip-curry chowder, either," she said to Barbara, naming one of the vegetarian delicacies for which Bon Mot was particularly known. "Just, like, chicken noodle and whatever else was lying around."

"Help yourself," Joe said. Heather retreated to the kitchen and returned with several wrapped packages. Joe felt an odd thrill of pleasure – it was so rare these days that he felt he was able to help her out without seeming to tread on her independence.

Father and daughter accompanied the caterers out to the curb and reiterated their thank-yous. "You take care, Joe," Barbara said as she got into her van. "Make sure you keep busy!"

"You read my mind," Joe called as she pulled away and rounded the cul-de-sac.

Almost immediately, Joe felt his energy begin to wane. He loved being around people, that was true, but after nearly five hours of being "on stage," he was also looking forward to the quiet round trip to Heather's house and then, to bed with his Kindle to finish the latest Nelson DeMille novel. He didn't want to stay up too late. He had a standing golf date with John Loughlin and a couple of other friends in the morning.

He turned on the BMW's radio as they hit the road, but his two favorite stations were playing commercials. All of his children had at one point or another told him that he needed to get an iPod adapter to hook into his car's stereo, or at least to install Pandora on his phone, but he hadn't gotten around to it. Maybe now, with his newfound free time…

He glanced at Heather. She was absorbed in her iPhone, thumbs working furiously.

"What are you doing now?" Joe asked.

"Posting a review," she said. "I don't think I told you about that horrible restaurant Julie and I went to, last Thursday?"

"No."

"Well, I did complain about it on Twitter," she said. "But since you don't use it yet, I guess you didn't see that!" Joe shot her a look. "Just teasing. Hang on," Heather said. "Let me just post this on Yelp." She took another few moments to read over what she'd written, then Joe heard the whooshing sound her phone made as she submitted her review. "It was so ridiculous, you wouldn't believe it," she said, not missing a beat. "I took Julie out to celebrate her getting her graduate degree? And then the roof started leaking?"

Joe had learned long ago not to take the upward inflection at the end of many of his kids' sentences as that of a question. He resisted the urge to insert, "Seriously?" which was one of Eric's favorite (and constant) expressions. "You didn't tell me about that yet," he said instead. "What happened?"

"So, we were eating, and the roof started leaking on our table. And this was a nice place, right – I mean, I'd made reservations there specially, and it was totally packed out with people."

"Well, it's been pretty rainy," Joe said. "They can't help that, I suppose."

"No, but wait," Heather said. "So we point out to the waiter that there is, like, water dripping right into our Caesar salad. And because they were so busy, they kicked us out into the lobby while they were getting a new table ready for us. For 20 minutes, at least. And they just, like, left us there. They didn't bring us our drinks or let us know what was going on, or anything."

Joe chuckled, picturing Heather and her friend stewing over the watery Caesar without even a beer to soothe their indignation. "That's pretty bad," he admitted.

"Dad, it gets way worse," Heather continued. "They finally were able to reseat us, and they got us a new salad and stuff. And I'll admit, the food was really good. I could see why they were so crowded even though they'd just opened. But anyway, we're about halfway through our entrées, and the waiter comes up to us to ask how everything is, and he sort of clears his throat. And Julie and I look up and he says, 'The owner would like to offer to split a dessert with you.' Split a dessert. That's the best they could offer us! So we kind of look at each other, because we don't usually even order dessert, and just kind of go, 'Okay, whatever.'"

"Could you tell who the owner was?" Joe asked.

"Oh, yeah. She was sort of hovering near the kitchen. Just kind of, I don't know, surveying the scene or whatever. You could tell she was important because of how all of the wait staff acted around her.

"So anyway, we finish dinner, and they bring over the dessert menu, and we decide to share something small and have coffee, you know? There were a couple of kinds of cannolis on the menu – the place was Italian – so we went ahead and ordered a chocolate cannoli and a couple of espressos."

"I still don't know how you can drink those at night," Joe said. "I'd be up until dawn if I took that much caffeine on board after dinner."

Heather laughed. "You've just got to build up a tolerance, Dad. I started in college; by now a chocolate cannoli and an espresso are practically like warm milk to me."

"So how was the cannoli?"

"That's the thing," Heather said. "You know how I said we never would have even ordered dessert if the owner hadn't oh-so-generously offered to 'split' it with us?" Joe nodded. "Well," Heather continued, "the cannoli was just a regular cannoli, you know. A couple of ounces of pastry and cream with chocolate drizzled on top. But – you're not going to believe this bit – the kitchen had actually cut the thing in half! As if they were saying, 'This is the half we are paying for.'"

Joe had to admit that was pretty outrageous. "You should have only eaten one half, maybe," he teased.

"And then when the bill comes," Heather said, "sure enough, she's charged us for half a cannoli. I mean, isn't that ridiculous?"

"I can't imagine they'll stay in business long, if that's the best they can do for customers that have been rained on," Joe said. "So you're writing a review?"

"Yeah, I already posted it to Yelp," Heather said. "But I'm going to do it on CitySearch, too. Do you use that site when you travel? You can see how well a hotel or restaurant or whatever is rated, based on user reviews."

Joe had seen such sites, but usually disregarded their ratings, preferring to go by word-of-mouth from people he knew. "Well, those must be skewed to the negative, right? I mean, most people probably write in when they're angry about something," he said.

"I've heard people say that," Heather said. "But if that's the case, then why are some places still getting four and five stars? I figure, it's a level playing field. Even if a lot of people write reviews when they're disgruntled, it should be the same percentage of negative reviews across the board."

Joe felt a glow of pride at his daughter's astuteness. "I hadn't thought about it that way," he said. "But I guess you're right. If a restaurant has five stars, that must mean that it hasn't served anyone half a cannoli in compensation for a wet Caesar salad – at least, not lately."

"You know there's a site like that for businesses too, don't you?" Heather asked. "Exact same concept."

"I hadn't heard that," Joe admitted.

"Yep. It's called Glassdoor.com. People submit reviews and ratings for their companies and even companies' executives. A lot of my friends are checking out the places they're applying to work before they even bother to send in a resume. You can tell a lot about a place by the number of people that bother to write reviews, and by the kind of reviews they get from employees… and maybe especially from ex-employees."

Joe mulled this over, thinking again how glad he had been about Ripen's policy of treating people well when he'd had to let Ed Burns go. He made a mental note to look up the site Heather was referencing later, and perhaps to submit a few reviews of his own. Not only of companies he had personally worked for, but perhaps also for executives who had been his clients over the years. He was sure that his experience would be of interest to people who might be considering working for some of those organizations.

That last thought tied in with a concept he had been kicking around during his last days at Ripen. He hadn't gotten it fully articulated, but it was coming together now. "You know," he said to Heather, "I'm sure you're tired of listening to me talk about business stuff tonight. But I just had a thought."

Heather had just been about to return to her phone, but she put it down in her lap for the second time that night. "Okay, Dad," she said. "I'll give you one more 'thought,' and then I'm going to make you talk about sports, or something. Sheesh, even golf."

"Don't kid a kidder, kid," Joe said. "I know you'd rather listen to me go on about business all night rather than talk about which iron I'm preferring these days on a particular hole."

"Fair enough," Heather said. "What's got you going now?"

"Recently, when I was working," Joe said, "one of the concepts I was piecing together was this 'co-branding' thing. At least, that's what I called it. Co-branding was all about companies understanding and promoting their product brand and their employment brand together. See, one of the key things I discovered was that one of the ways you build or sustain a successful company is to hire the kinds of people who are likely to succeed in your company. It always surprised me how few companies do that."

"Like Southwest Airlines," Heather said. "You mentioned them during your speech tonight, when you were talking about 'Why' and 'Why not.'"

"How do you mean?" Joe asked.

"Well, think about why people choose to fly Southwest. It's not just because they don't charge for luggage or whatever. It's also because they're kind of more fun than other airlines, right? I mean, last time I flew to L.A., one of the flight attendants sang a song while we were landing – some cute thing he'd made up about Hollywood. He didn't have a bad voice, either."

"Exactly," Joe said. "Maybe you should have been a management consultant yourself! Part of their brand is fun, so they attract and hire fun employees. Right?" Heather smiled, clearly pleased that she'd anticipated where her Dad was going. "But you bring up an interesting point with these online reviews that you were talking about." She looked instantly quizzical. Joe guessed that, since such things came as second nature to her, she might not view them in as groundbreaking a light as he did. After all, if her friends could instantly and easily research an organization they were considering applying for, she might also take for granted the implications for those organizations themselves. "You and your technology toys are able to communicate your opinions about all this stuff instantaneously to your friends, and they to their friends," he said, nudging her.

"Dad, I'm not just communicating to my friends. Millions of people I don't know read this stuff," Heather said.

"And that's exactly my point," Joe replied. "So from an organizational perspective, those little devices are really *brand accelerators.*"

Heather paused to think this over before adding, "Or decelerators, if the reviews are bad."

"Exactly," Joe said. He suddenly wondered how ThinkSmart was rated on the site Heather had mentioned, and made a mental note to find out.

Heather was watching him. After what she apparently deemed to be a sufficient lapse in the conversation, she picked up her phone again. A quick glance confirmed that she was updating her Facebook profile. Within a minute, Joe could hear the tinny sound of an online video emitting from the passenger seat.

YouTube. Now there was a potential brand accelerator. Joe remembered a Ripen meeting he had participated in with a new client. Venerable sneaker company Viakix had found itself in the unexpected yet enviable position of enjoying a surge of popularity among customers in their 20s. (Previously, their flagship shoe was best known as the walking sneaker of choice for the nursing-home set.) *Funny*, Joe had thought at the time, *the things kids pick up and made fashionable again.* Viakix's CEO, Paul Fennelly, had turned to Ripen's marketing division for help exploring this new market. Joe, as the Ripen client liaison, had been included in the meeting.

About fifteen minutes into a discussion about advertising tactics, a junior member of Viakix's team spoke up. "Scrap television and radio," Drew Costello had said. "We ought to be doing YouTube shorts if we want to reach that demographic." "That demographic," in this case, was comprised of kids not much younger than Drew himself. He was a recent college graduate from Salem State University who, Joe knew, had only been invited to the meeting as part of the company's "Reach for the Stars" program, which recognized high-potential junior members by bringing them to the table with senior management.

Everyone at the table had turned to Paul Fennelly. With his thick white hair and piercing black eyes, he was an imposing figure. Frankly, Joe had been utterly shocked that Drew had the guts to say anything at all. He'd watched the CEO's still-black eyebrows draw toward his nose in what could most leniently be described as skepticism (a scowl was a closer match). "I've been in this business a long time," he said curtly. "You don't sell products on YouTube. That's completely the wrong venue, especially for our clientele. It's free entertainment, for starters. What are we going to do, have a singing and dancing kitten sell our shoes?"

There were a few stifled laughs around the table. Fascinated by the kid's creativity, Joe was about to speak up in Drew's defense, but it seemed that Drew didn't need his help. "What do we have to lose?" Drew said, cool and collected. "The cost is minimal – the cost of production."

Paul Fennelly was regarding Drew evenly. He seemed about to say something else dismissive, but Joe took the opportunity to quietly say, "You might as well see if it works, Paul. If it doesn't, you can always go back to radio or TV. Drew is right; these things can be made quickly."

"And they have a whole level of exposure that traditional media lacks," ventured the director of Viakix's West Coast manufacturing. "It doesn't have to be dancing kittens, either."

"It should be funny, though," Drew said. "Generally speaking, that's the best approach if you aren't going to be raunchy. Maybe even use footage or voiceovers of customers talking about the new shoe."

The older members of the executive team appeared to be considering the idea with new gravity now that Drew had the CEO's attention. "Whom would you recommend we work with, to create such an ad?" Joe asked.

"You know Dom and Damfan?" Drew said. "Why not them?"

Paul Fennelly snorted. "Isn't that just a couple of kids in a dorm room?"

"Maybe so," Joe had said, glad to support the idea. "But even *I* know those guys' ads. Heck, I probably get one of their spots forwarded to me once a month by my daughter."

In the BMW, he stole another look out of the corner of his eye at Heather. The light from her phone played over her features; there was a small smile on her lips as she nodded in appreciation of whatever it was she was watching. It might even have been another of the Viakix ads that had been the end result of the meeting he'd been recalling. The original spot, featuring Puggle puppies that used the new sneakers like pogo sticks, had gone viral – everyone, it appeared, had forwarded the link to their friends. And those friends had told other friends about it. A series of ads had followed; the shoes themselves were eventually referred to as "Puggles" rather than by their original, somewhat boring product name, "Volts." The last Joe had seen, there was even a mobile app – a game where you bounced the puppies themselves into the sneakers. Soon people were playing it on the subway.

It wouldn't surprise me if that was Drew's idea too, Joe thought. If that kid hadn't been in that meeting, none of it would have happened. Viakix would probably have gone right back to being old people's walking shoes once the Volts fad faded.

He turned down the lane to his daughter's house for the second time that night. His brain, which had been looking forward to bed and a book not so long ago, was now racing with new thoughts. *We used to talk about diversity*, was one of these. *But I guess that doesn't just mean having people from different ethnic backgrounds anymore. Generational diversity might even be* **more** *important… diversity is as much about innovation as it is equality!*

"Here we are," he said to Heather. "Thanks again for coming along."

"I enjoyed it, Dad," Heather said, leaning over to give him a peck on the cheek. "Happy retirement. I'm so proud of what you've accomplished! Why don't you start off with a leisurely morning tomorrow?"

Joe smiled and watched her until she had disappeared into her own apartment and the door was safely closed behind her. He didn't have the heart to tell her that part of him was dreading leisure, although he was looking forward to that golf game tomorrow. Driving home, he wondered whether it was the game itself that seemed so appealing at the moment, or the opportunity to continue gathering grist for the concept that had been taking shape in his head over the past few weeks, which, to his surprise, had become even more solid in the past few hours. For starters, a concept he was beginning to think of as tri-branding was now crystalizing in his head.

If co-branding represents the linkage with one's employment and product brand, he thought, *tri-branding leverages social media (the ultimate brand accelerator) to add a third link –* the connection with one's customers, vendors, applicants, former employees, and other key stakeholders so that they become brand ambassadors.

As Joe drove away, he wrestled with one pressing question. *What makes for great, sustainable cultures and business models?* he asked himself. He had a feeling his "recipe" was still missing one or two ingredients. Beyond that, he was preoccupied with renewed doubts about his decision to retire. *It feels as if I'm on the cusp of understanding something important,* he thought. *If I'm right, it's too big not to share.*

Global Growth

Joe woke early the next morning after a somewhat fitful night. The detective novel had languished; he hadn't been able to keep his mind on the plot. He'd gotten up several times to jot down notes and doodle. And he'd made the mistake of poking around on the Internet, looking at some of the sites Heather had been talking about – and after a certain hour, he'd noticed, almost any time spent in front of the computer kept him awake. This wasn't exactly how he'd pictured the first "official" day of his retirement. But he recognized in himself the stirring of new ideas, and he'd learned long ago to invite them in. *At least I won't be bored, being retired,* he thought, pulling a razor over his face in the steamy, seven-AM bathroom. *I just am going to have to be sure I don't drive everyone else crazy, talking about business ideas now that I'm supposed to be out of the game.*

That said, he did want to share some of his late-night musings with Heather – after all, she'd gotten his gears going in a lot of ways. He waited until what he thought was an acceptably late hour, then called her. It went to voice mail. "Hi, honey," he said. "Hope you got some sleep last night. I read your restaurant review – did you see there are already three more? Anyway, give me a call. I gotta share something with you."

The second he hung up, his phone bleeped with a text from Heather. "What?"

He dialed her again. Maddeningly, the phone rang until it went to voice mail. It was Sunday; he was pretty sure she had a yoga class to go to, which was why he'd felt okay about calling her before nine. But she wouldn't be texting from yoga class, would she? He hung up and re-accessed her terse message, glowing up at him. Somewhat awkwardly, he began to type. He hadn't quite gotten the hang of his phone's touch screen. It astounded him that his sons, whose fingers were without question larger than his, managed it as easily as breathing. "Did you get my voice mail?" he finally tapped out, and sent.

Not even three seconds passed. "No. What?"

He debated phoning again, but remembered, with some humor, that his daughter's generation refused to listen to voice mails. So he texted back. "Do you have a minute? Please call me."

A moment later, his phone rang. He answered it while pouring himself a bowl of cereal – his stomach had started growling, and he'd briefly debated digging in to some of the catering leftovers before reminding himself to get off on the right foot in the dietary sense.

"Morning," Heather said. She sounded as if she were halfway through breakfast herself; he could hear her chewing. "What's up, Dad? Don't tell me: you've come up with a million-dollar idea just since last night."

Joe grinned. "Not quite. But I did do a lot of thinking."

"Of course you did," Heather said, teasing again. "Anyone who thought you'd be taking up chess or some other new hobby when you retired obviously doesn't know my workaholic Dad."

Given his occasional misgivings about being so focused on work while the kids were growing up, that stung just a little. But he wanted to make sure Heather knew she had been the one to set him off on the new line of thinking that was beginning to seem really exciting to him. "Well, remember that conversation we had last night when I was driving you home? Where we sort of worked out that social media was a brand accelerator?"

"Uh-huh," Heather said, crunching down on whatever it was she was eating.

"Well, I'm sure you remember the Viakix sneakers. My involvement with that," Joe said.

"Puggles! Sure I remember," Heather said. "It was pretty cool to be able to tell my friends that you'd worked on that. A lot of the kids at Beacon Communities still rock those shoes."

Joe allowed himself a momentary rush of satisfaction, then charged ahead. "I'm afraid I can't really take credit for those ads with the puppies," he said. "It was a guy about your age that came up with the campaign. I just argued for it with Viakix's executives."

"Well, whoever was responsible pretty much hit a home run," Heather said. "I heard there's actually some kind of

PuggleBounce theme park under construction in Japan! You know, based on that mobile app."

A theme park based on a mobile phone game that was itself based on a YouTube ad campaign, Joe thought. In Japan, no less. *Well, I suppose stranger things have happened.* "That actually fits right in to the idea that was keeping me up last night," he said. "What's happened with Viakix and those Volt sneakers, or Puggles. That's no longer just co-branding. It's more like... tri-branding. It's what every company ought to be aspiring to. Leaders need to understand that to sustain their brand in today's marketplace, they need to somehow enlist their customers – and their customers' customers, and their customers' co-workers, and friends, and families – as ambassadors for the brand."

"You mean, getting all those people playing PuggleBounce to do their work for them?" Heather asked.

"In a sense, yes," Joe said. "It's like Apple aficionados. Pretty much every time I want to show off some feature on my phone, there's someone with an iPhone handy, just waiting to trump whatever it is I'm excited about. Apple has managed to achieve not just brand loyalty, but brand ambassadorship. Their customers are out there recruiting new customers! Apple's sales organization is really every Apple customer. And it's funny, they were the same way when the Mac was losing the PC war to IBM compatibles. Their brand passion is contagious, and with social media, smart businesses will realize they need to leverage this new highway of communication and connectivity! Am I making any sense here, on a Sunday morning?"

Heather laughed. "Yes, Dad, you are. And now that you mention it, I also tend to get great satisfaction sharing things I like with others. It's like being in on a good thing that you want to spread around."

"Exactly," Joe said. "Those YouTube ads... the way they went viral... well, it shocked a lot of us, including Viakix's executives. And they already pretty much had the co-branding thing going on. Their employment brand was linked with their 'sneaker' brand. They had high levels of employee engagement. You could have asked virtually any member of that company, from the shoe designers to the manufacturing line managers, what it was that they were doing... and they'd confidently recite Viakix's mission statement. More than that; they'd say they *believed* in it. At the time when I worked with them, the company was actively pursuing new ways to engage their staff, with social and environmental sustainability measures that Ripen helped them put together. But it wasn't until the brand took root with their customers – with those silly, infectious puppy ads – that Viakix managed to hit that next branding level."

"Tri-branding, huh?" Heather asked. "It sounds like something one of my environmental scientist friends talks about. Like, a catalyst for exponential growth. Or… what is the other thing he always talks about… *propagation of a meme.* You know it was an evolutionary biologist who first came up with the meme thing, right?"

Joe had known that, although he'd admit the term had puzzled him at first. "I do pay attention every once in a while, Heather," he asserted. "You don't need to be a scientist to know that a meme is an idea, behavior, or style that spreads from person to person. And you're right; tri-branding is very much the same, the way I'm conceptualizing it." He thought for a moment, staring at the still-dry cereal he'd poured. On the phone, it sounded as if Heather had just bitten into an apple.

"I wanted to thank you this morning, I guess," he said. "It was really you and your phone, and your restaurant review that made some of this stuff fall into place for me. At my party, I was talking about how to create a sustainable business, right? Well, what better way to do that than by leveraging technology to connect with your clients to reach that third level of branding?"

Heather munched her fruit, "Wow," she said. "I guess… glad to have helped? I don't think I really did anything, though."

"Trust me, you did," Joe said. "I love you, sweetheart."

"Love you too, Dad. Listen," she said after a pause. "I really do want you to have some fun today. But I have to say, I can't remember when I last saw you this excited about anything work-related. Um… you sure this retiring thing is a good idea?"

Joe chuckled – Heather had a knack for reading his mind. "Well, there's only one way to find out," he said. "I'm playing golf with John, Eduardo, and Kathy today, so I guess I'll see if a 'life of leisure' is as appealing as it seemed when I had my nose to the grindstone." He glanced at the clock. "As a matter of fact, I oughtta hit the road. It's later than I realized."

"Well, I'm about to be late for yoga," Heather replied. "So – please enjoy yourself! I plan to."

"Thanks. I'm looking forward to it," Joe said, thinking

that his reasons for the anticipation were maybe not quite what Heather would assume. "I'll talk to you soon."

"Love you, Dad," Heather said again, and hung up.

Joe pressed "End Call" on his phone, still feeling keyed up. He was sure he was on to something that would have been his next "big idea" as a management consultant. Surely, his burgeoning ideas about creativity, question-asking, innovation, and branding were parts of a real, workable model for organizations. As of now, he was resolved to continue to cultivate these thoughts. Perhaps he was not yet done contributing to the ongoing discussion about business sustainability.

Still nursing these preoccupations, Joe changed into his golfing clothes, gathered his clubs, and headed for the course. He'd arranged to meet his friends at the clubhouse at 10 AM, and they didn't disappoint him. John Loughlin, Joe's neighbor and the resident sports hero, was already there, looking as hale and formidable as ever. Although Joe had by now settled into a comfortable friendship with John, he couldn't help feeling a slight, star-struck thrill at the prospect of golfing with the Rattlers' manager. Compactly built and with a blasé expression that was difficult to crack, John had the air of a man who "owned" his successes and acknowledged his failures with equal commitment. In his years of consulting, Joe had rarely seen such self-awareness, and he admired John all the more for not letting it go to his head. It had paid off; it was well-known that for the last 10 years, under John's leadership, the Rattlers had held the best winning percentage in the history of the National Football League.

They had barely said hello before they were joined by Eduardo Lopes, the sales director of international real estate development company Vargas Perdillo. Joe had met Eduardo on this very golf course. Following Eduardo closely and wearing a determined expression that Joe knew to take seriously, was Kathy Barnett. Kathy usually golfed with her husband, Art, with whom she also worked with at Confident Care, a major healthcare organization. But she'd let "the guys" know that although Art was travelling, she'd still be there to tee off on Sunday, and was thankful that Joe's group had an opening in their foursome. "Gotta keep learning the game," she said as she approached. "I know you'll be kind to me." This last line was delivered with a wink; everyone present knew that Kathy was already a competitive golfer.

Joe savored the morning calm, and the focus he was able to bring to his opening drive. He knew not to read too much into the first few strokes, but he was pleased with himself thus far. It was John who broke the silence, with the requisite retirement joke about how much Joe's game was benefiting.

"I doubt a couple of days of retirement will have helped that much," Joe said. "Give me at least until the sixth hole before appointing me Tiger."

"We'll just see about that," Kathy put in. Petite, with piercing brown eyes, Kathy was the youngest member of the group and was careful to assert herself where and when she could. She was more than a decade younger than her husband, Art, but had already virtually overtaken him at Confident Care. Kathy had achieved the position of director of training and organizational development for Confident Care in the last year or so. Her expertise was wide-ranging, and she made sure anyone who was prone to mistake her for a "newbie" was quickly corrected. Her drive, almost predictably, landed within feet of Joe's.

Enjoying deep breaths of the cool morning air and the

first touch of the day's sun on his arms, Joe was almost sorry when John asked, "So, how is retirement?" as they were teeing off the second tee. He followed John's slice off the fairway with one of his own before answering.

"You know, I'm already questioning if I'm going to be a 'retirement' kind of guy." The thought of retirement was beginning to gnaw at him in increasing ways. Fundamentally, he felt that he still had much to offer, especially given his revelations over the past 24 hours. Perhaps his "Boomer conscience" was already nagging at him, too, reminding him there was still work to be done even if he'd earned a bit of rest. "It was great seeing so many old colleagues last night," he told John as they walked toward the third hole. "Reminded me of so much – maybe *too* much – of my life's work, all in one night. It's a little mind-boggling, how much people and business have evolved." Suddenly aware that this might seem gloomy, Joe added lightheartedly, "Not that that's anything you'd have to worry about. As the Rattlers' manager, I imagine things are pretty cut-and-dry. I mean, professional football is a game, and that's not apt to change, is it?"

John Loughlin fussed with his golf bag, vacillating between two different clubs. "Managing a football team isn't so different from managing a business," he said after a moment. He selected a club and tested its weight with a few experimental swings. "I have players, like any company has employees. And I have to maximize their productivity, commitment, and effort. I have to innovate my playbook, to differentiate from other teams." He turned his frank blue gaze toward Joe. "Really, it's no different than your clients' having to differentiate themselves from the competition. We're both trying to balance the need for short-term wins against the goal of long-term, sustainable success."

Joe was a little discomfited by how close to the mark John had hit. "Are you sure you weren't recording my little speech last night?" he joked. "Also, who are you kidding? You can't tell me that you're not focused on trying to win this season!" At Joe's right, Kathy and Eduardo elbowed one another.

"Earlier in my career, I felt like that," John said. "Perhaps more so when I didn't have the same level of confidence or job security that I do today. But what I've learned with the Rattlers is that creating a sustained level of performance is how I will be measured. And that means making really tough decisions sometimes. Like letting some of my veteran players sign elsewhere so that I can introduce some of my new players into starting roles. So I'm doing succession planning, too." John threw Kathy a wink with this last comment; succession planning was a big part of her new role.

Without comment, Joe located his four-iron. He swung, and shanked the ball yards to the right of the green. "Dammit," he couldn't help muttering.

Eduardo lofted his ball and dropped a beautiful five-iron drive off the side of the green. It was going to be a close game.

The foursome meandered toward their balls. The morning was almost absurdly beautiful. Birds were singing someplace to the east of the fairway, and the sun illuminated each closely tended blade of grass and glinted off the leaves in the surrounding trees. *I guess I could get used to this*, Joe thought. *If only it were enough.*

"I've always said that businesses have to be sustainable," he said to John. "For a company to succeed, its leaders have to take care of today, but make sure they are investing in tomorrow. I guess in sports, too, that means somehow creating a culture of growth and experimentation."

John chuckled. "Maybe I should have hired you as my defensive coordinator," he said. "I've always tried to teach my guys as well as the team's owners that our players need to grow, our schemes need to be more creative, and we have to outsmart our competition."

Joe was still a bit taken aback at the similarities John was describing. It was hard to accept that someone as cool and collected as John could have faced the same challenges Joe had helped clients tackle for years. "Come on, now," he said. "The Rattlers have been one of the most successful teams in the league for a long time! You must have it down to a science by now."

John looked thoughtful. "These days," he said, "the biggest challenge for all of us, both coaches and managers, is understanding the younger players and learning how to relate to them. They just think differently than we think." Joe found himself nodding enthusiastically, and thinking how many of his friends, colleagues, and clients would understand what John was saying. What the Rattlers' manager said next also resonated with Joe: "Sometimes I think it's time for me to let some of the younger guys step up and take over," John mused.

"But it's because of knowing that some time it's going to be best for the team that I bow out, I've spent quite a bit of time putting in a system that will be sustainable well after I leave."

There was a resolute note in John's voice that reminded Joe of how he'd sounded, figuring out whom at Ripen should take on the responsibilities he was vacating. *I wonder if it's the same for a lot of us Boomers*, he thought. *Delegating responsibilities can feel a lot like writing your last will and testament, no matter how silly that seems to younger folks, or how impatient they are to get on with things.* He shook his head. "Forget me joining your team," he said to John. "I should've had some of my clients hire you. Creating a business model that can sustain itself during and after transition is the mark of a great leader."

John gave him an appreciative but skeptical squint. "Coming from anyone but you, that'd just sound like you were blowing smoke," he said.

A loud cry of "Fore!" interrupted them. Kathy's errant fairway shot missed John by a mere couple of feet.

"Sorry!" Kathy shouted, approaching them. "You looked like you were having such a good time – I guess I just had to interrupt." Although to a casual bystander this might have sounded like a joke, Joe knew Kathy well enough to guess that there was more than a grain of truth in it. Likely, she'd been watching him and John closely, and had gleaned that there was a conversation happening that might interest her. After all, Kathy hadn't gotten where she was by ignoring any business lesson – even, or maybe especially, the kind that originated on the golf course.

Joe decided to invite her into the discussion. "John and I were just talking about needing to have a culture that is sustainable beyond its current leadership," he said, "whether that's in a business selling flowerpots, or a sports team."

Kathy laughed. "I should have figured you guys would be talking shop," she said. "Of course you know that topic is interesting to me, right?"

Joe gave Kathy a warm smile. "Of course. Training Director at Confident Care, now, aren't you?"

"That's right: its Training and Organizational Development Director," Kathy corrected, leaning on her club. "As John mentioned earlier, succession planning is a huge issue for us right now. We've got leaders throughout Confident Care who are very, very good at what they do. But the problem is that our investment in developing future leaders is way too light. It's treated almost as an afterthought."

"I'm familiar with that approach," Joe said.

"Or lack of one, you mean to say," Kathy rejoined. "Sometimes, I just don't think our leadership wants to face the fact that sometime they're going to have to retire – unless of course they die on the job!" Here, both Joe and John winced at Kathy's characteristic bluntness. She was so pixie-like, with that wicked twinkle in her eye, that they immediately felt a little foolish for doing so. "My point is, guys –" here Kathy paused for effect – "it takes a secure leader to develop his or her successor. And those choices have to be made very carefully. Most importantly, you can't assume that just because someone is great in their job, they will be great in their manager's job. The vast majority of high-performing employees are not succession candidates for their manager's job."

She put a palm to her brow and scanned the course for Eduardo. He'd gotten stuck in the rough, and was now letting another group play through. Kathy gave him a quick wave to let him know they would wait for him. She then turned back to Joe and John and leaned on her club. "Here's a recent example," she said. "We had a nurse... I'll call her Sally. She was at the top of her game in pediatrics – I mean, not only did her patients rave about her, but their families did too. Her name came up all the time in other nurses' reviews. She was one of those natural mentors, you know? The kind of person that's just sort of quietly inspiring by doing what they do best."

Joe nodded. He thought he knew the type. Sometimes these were the shyest, most retiring sorts, too: people who had found their natural groove, sometimes off the regular career track.

"But what happened," Kathy continued, "was that when the head pediatric nurse retired, everyone assumed that Sally ought to take her place. The assumption everyone made – and I'm not exempt here, guys, I thought the same thing – was that because she was a great nurse, she'd make a great manager."

"Thanks for letting that group behind us hit through," Eduardo said, joining them. "I'm afraid it took me four strokes to get out of there," he added. "This is certainly not going to go down as my greatest game! But I've interrupted," he said, turning back to Kathy with the suggestion of a bow. The gesture might have seemed affected coming from anyone but Eduardo. With his scrupulously kept curly coif and sideburns,

Eduardo carried himself with a courtly air that seemed to extend naturally to even his most casual interactions.

"Not at all," Kathy said. "I was just telling them about the lesson I learned with Sally – you know. We discussed it over dinner when Art and I had you and Rochelle over last time." Eduardo demurred with another courtly nod, and Kathy continued her story. "So, we promoted Sally. Maybe you see where this is going?"

John and Joe both shook their heads, although Joe had a pretty good idea. "As we ultimately found out, she wasn't management material by a long shot," Kathy concluded. "She pretty much alternated between micro-managing or being way too hands-off. She'd try to enforce methods that had worked for her personally, but she was so conflict-averse that when an issue came up, she sort of threw up her hands. And that's leaving aside the fact that since so many of 'her' nurses were old friends… Sally tended to take their side even when there were things that clearly needed to change, way too often."

Eduardo added some context. "This was just as Kathy was beginning her role as Lead Training Director," he said. "So she had her plate full from the very first day."

Kathy drew her shoulders back, looking a little defensive.

"Training and Organizational Director," she corrected again. "Well, I think that situation would have been challenging for anybody, no matter how long they'd been on the job," she said. She then seemed almost immediately to remember that she was among friends and relaxed, tilting her golf club off to one side like a dancer's prop cane. "Anyway," she said, "Sally and I had a long discussion. We really focused on her strengths, and finding the places where they overlapped with Confident Care's goals. It seemed to come as a relief to her, actually, that someone finally asked whether she wanted to be a manager. Because she didn't!"

It seemed an appropriate time to continue to golf, so the four players concentrated on getting up to the green. Joe teased Eduardo for sandbagging his handicap; he'd not only managed to catch up, but had taken over the lead, even with his trouble getting out of the rough. As they played, Kathy continued to recount Sally's story; apparently, Kathy had brought in a new manager for the pediatric ward, allowing a grateful Sally to go back to what she did best. However, Kathy said, she'd found a new outlet for Sally's talents: teaching her best client-service techniques to incoming staff. "This way," Kathy said triumphantly, "Everyone got the best out of the situation."

By this time, Joe was really ready to eat. That morning's healthy breakfast might have been the best thing for his waistline, but after a morning of fresh air, golf, and food for thought, he was ready for a sandwich. John continued to josh Eduardo a bit about his "surprise" victory. "Quit pretending," he growled. "We all know that in Brazil, all you did was play golf!"

"I guess the weather allowed you to play year-round," Joe piled on, aware that he was opening himself up for a counter-attack about his retirement allowing him to play year-round, too.

They arrived at the clubhouse and were seated in good time; the place was uncharacteristically quiet for a Sunday. Looking around, Joe reflected that it wasn't what his father might have expected in a golf club. It was considerably more ethnically diverse, a fact that was even reflected in the choices available on the menu. And while Kathy was the only woman in the club today, that tended to be a fairly rare occurrence, with female players often occupying whole booths and enjoying some passionate game recaps. *One thing most of us have in common is being over 50,* Joe thought to himself, before remembering that Eduardo was considerably younger.

Joe was famished, but mindful that he shouldn't order the first thing that jumped out at him. Although he could easily have eaten twice as much, he opted for a half-tuna sandwich and salad, rather than the chorizo clam chowder and steak-and-cheese Hoagie that had immediately tempted him. Engrossed momentarily in patting himself on the back for a more heart-healthy choice, Joe missed out on the others' conversation for a few moments. As his attention was re-focused, he was glad that he'd been seated with his back to the windows facing out onto the golf course; the light streaming through them would have made it difficult for him to see his friends' faces. As it was, Kathy and John's profiles stood out sharply in the bright noon sunlight, and Eduardo's animated face was as brightly lit as if he'd been in a movie studio.

"Rochelle is an American," he was saying, as if this explained a deep truth about his wife. He brushed a wayward black curl from his forehead. "She wanted to return home. So I came here to follow my wife's career."

Competitive as always, John seemed unable to let the gibe about the game die a natural death. "That's why you're so good at golf," he said, swirling the ice in his water. "Apparently you don't work!"

"Of course I work," Eduardo said, laughing good-naturedly. "But in my line of work, it doesn't matter where I or my 200 employees sit."

"That's true," John and Joe conceded, almost in unison. Vargas Perdillo, the company for which Eduardo was General Manager, was beginning to crop up in global media as a major player in real estate development. The company's reach had expanded to encompass Latin America and parts of Germany, and its mixed-use and transit-oriented developments were attracting a previously untapped market of upwardly mobile, technologically savvy young professionals who commuted to city centers from poorer communities.

"I fell in love with my wife when she was visiting São Paulo on business," Eduardo said earnestly to Kathy. "It was obvious that her line of work would not allow her to relocate. To be honest, I wasn't sure mine would, either. The majority of my employees are in São Paulo." He looked around the table, engaging Joe and John in turn. Joe couldn't help but acknowledge that it couldn't be an easy decision to leave behind your country and your native language. It would take a tremendous amount of courage, confidence, and optimism.

And, he thought, *I'd somehow taken all that for granted. I've never heard what happened!*

"What the heck did you tell them?" Kathy was asking, sparing Joe the trouble. The "them" in question was, apparently, Eduardo's management team: he was telling Kathy about how he had managed the move to the U.S.

"I told them, I am here with a dilemma," Eduardo said. "I have fallen in love with an American business woman, and I've made a decision to move to America to be with her." It was hard not to get a little misty about such a declaration; a glance around the table reassured Joe that he wasn't the only one affected. But despite his tall, dark, and handsome charm, Eduardo didn't seem to be relating this experience simply for sympathy, or to make a romantic impression. In fact, he seemed intent on relating the meeting just as he remembered it.

"I understood the hardship this would cause the business and I was prepared to step down, but I hoped we could find a workable solution to my dilemma," Eduardo said. "Yes, that is what I told them." He looked around the table. "And… you may not believe me… they laughed!"

At this inopportune moment, their salads arrived.

It took a moment of accepting freshly ground pepper and assuring their waiter that everything was satisfactory before Eduardo could resume.

"They laughed, you said," Joe prompted, digging into his greens and vinaigrette.

"They did," Eduardo said. "Frankie, my director of commercial leasing: he said, 'You scared me! I thought you were calling us together for something serious!'" And then he said, 'Expanding into America is inevitable.' He said, 'In our kind of business, it is no longer important where you sit. 'The world is flat, and in our world, growth means global growth,' he said."

Having all read Thomas Friedman's popular book of that same title, Joe, Kathy, and John all rewarded this disclosure with appreciative chuckles. "Indeed," Kathy said. Eduardo took a large bite of his Caesar with anchovies and chewed, looking around the table and savoring the agreement. "In this world of telecommuting, technology, and virtual workforces, it doesn't matter where you sit," he said when he had swallowed and wiped his mouth with the corner of his napkin. "What I learned from taking that chance... that chance that Rochelle made me take... was that Vargas Perdillo wanted a global presence.

And I was giving them a…" he paused, seeming to search for the right English word. The dark eyes lit up. "A foothold in a geography that we wanted anyways." Eduardo beamed around the table.

"You see, we had talked about wanting to have global exposure," he continued. "The younger generation – " here Eduardo was subjected to some groans from his tablemates, as he was the youngest present – "the younger generation is already travelling and studying abroad, at younger and younger ages! You know this," he exhorted. "Once upon a time, companies considered global expansion for market, customer, or cost reasons. Tomorrow, I predict the big driver of global expansion will be winning the war for talent. This so-called Generation Y wants to travel and work for global companies. Plus there are millions if not billions of potential employees in Brazil, China, India…"

"Yes, I know," Joe affirmed. All three of his children had already had opportunities, through university or through work, to spend considerable time in Europe and Asia. Heather had vacationed in Morocco while an undergraduate, actually, finding a chance to exercise her French while learning some Arabic and Berber. And although he had initially been resistant to Donna's insistence that Eric, their youngest, take Mandarin rather than Spanish, he had to admit that the payoff was looking substantial. Eric had quickly learned a language spoken by a part of the world that was increasingly integrated with his own. But Joe was also convinced that something about written Chinese had informed Eric's artistic direction. More than once, Joe remembered, he'd commented on the "pictorial" nature of Chinese characters... only, of course, to have one or another of his children correct him. "Logographic, Dad, not pictorial. There's a difference."

Joe's attention had wandered a bit, but Eduardo was still engrossing John and Kathy. "It was a thing they had aspired to," he was saying. "Without meaning to, I had given them an opportunity. And now, being here in the U.S., Vargas Perdillo is able to say that we, too, are global. We have an American address, and an American presence."

John was shaking his head, but in a way that somehow meant he was agreeing with Eduardo. "We know in America that what we call 'soccer' is 'football,' everywhere else," he said. "But it takes something like the Olympics to really get us thinking about global competition... even about something as universal as sports. Even the National Football League now schedules games overseas. Remember the exhibition game we played in Mexico last year?"

Joe instantly made a connection to Viakix – not surprising, given that the company had been on his mind for the past 24 hours more or less constantly. "In the last five years," he said, "more and more of my clients' business has been global. So many companies used to look at China or India as the manufacturing arm of their business, but as those countries have become developed, markets locally are opening up." Joe glanced at Eduardo, whose attention he seemed to have captured.

Kathy jumped in to share a recent experience. "Once, on a flight from Hong Kong to Shanghai, sitting beside me was Andrew 'Flip' Filipowski, CEO of SilkRoad Technologies. It wasn't a long flight, obviously, but we started chatting. And he explained his company's growth strategy in Asia," she said. "Flip told me that SilkRoad would make a lot more money if they just focused on U.S. growth. But for a cloud-based HR software company like SilkRoad to survive, they have to establish a global footprint to be relevant over time."

Joe chimed in, "In other words, SilkRoad is willing

to sacrifice today's profits for tomorrow's growth. That's sustainability!"

"And it's not just US companies, Eduardo added. "Executives outside the U.S. are now doing the same sort of expansion, including recruiting and establishing retail functions in the States, is that not correct?"

"That's absolutely correct," Joe said. "It's like you said. If 'the world is flat...' that doesn't just mean we can outsource more cheaply, or efficiently. It means that new markets are opening up. So the companies that are employing globally, also have the potential to sell globally." This entire conversation was, in its own way, underscoring Joe's ideas about tri-branding. He had to fight to keep from seeming overly excited about a conversation that his golfing partners were likely taking as the usual water-cooler chat they tended to exchange when playing.

The foursome's main courses arrived, and they all dug in with good appetite. The conversation turned to movies, but Joe's wheels were still turning. He was pretty sure they'd found, as Eduardo had said, "a foothold."

Creativeship

Two months had passed. As he sipped his iced tea, Joe could hear the auditorium filling up. As the newest addition to the speaker slate for the International Executive Leadership Council (IELC), he had been scheduled at an early and unpropitious hour: just before noon, when some of his audience would have no doubt slipped out for lunch, and the remainder would be preoccupied by rumbling stomachs. Joe was determined to capture their flagging attention as best he could. Although this was his first time presenting his "Creativeship" ideas, in the months since his retirement party he had distilled it down to some principles of which he felt very proud. He also felt energized, and keyed up by the possibility that this talk might mark his professional resurrection.

It wasn't that he hadn't enjoyed retirement. His golf game had improved considerably – he was now reliably giving Eduardo a run for his money. He'd finished every novel his favorite detective writer had ever written. He'd made some improvements to the landscape surrounding his new house. His oldest son, Stephen, was now on track to become a partner at the environmental law firm where he worked, and had gotten engaged. Joe had had the distinct pleasure of seeing Eric, his younger son, graduate from college. And he continued to enjoy his periodic outings with Heather. She had become a wonderful sounding board for him as he was putting together his ideas for a new kind of leadership. And she had been very supportive of his decision to begin marketing those ideas… a process that, for all intents and purposes, was bringing him out of retirement and back into the fray.

Joe also had to give credit to Eric, his younger son, who convinced Joe that traditional PowerPoint presentations put people to sleep. Eric's words are still echoing in his head. "You like to doodle. You communicate well like that. So why not just get those doodles up on a big screen as you draw them? Stick in some pictures, use multiple projectors to keep people awake, and you'll be good to go, Dad." He felt a rush of gratitude, knowing that Eric was sitting in the first row and would be controlling the slides for the second projector. They'd rehearsed several times; Joe was pretty sure they had it down pat.

"Mr. Daniels?" An event coordinator stuck his head into the small prep space where Joe was standing in the back of the auditorium. "Everything's set for you."

"Thanks," Joe said, smoothing his pants. He took a deep breath. *Think of it as one of your practice sessions with Heather,* he thought. *This is no different, really; if it needs fine-tuning, this is the only way to find out.*

He waited in the rear as he was introduced. The man giving the introduction was Michael Porter, Chairman of the Board of the IELC. Michael sounded a bit sleepy; Joe was sure he had been up since very early this morning. But he got through the specifics of Joe's credentials and got a little life into his presentation as he concluded. "Without further ado, then, may I present Mr. Joe Daniels!"

The lights dimmed to complete darkness. A single spotlight shone on the stage's podium. There was an audible inhalation from the audience, and the sound of collective shifting in chairs. Suddenly, a second spotlight appeared at the back of the auditorium, illuminating Joe. "Ladies and gentlemen, I'm here to announce that leadership is dead," Joe began as he walked slowly toward the podium.

As Joe stepped out, the house lights came up slightly, remaining dim. To inquisitive applause, he made his way to the podium, where a tablet computer and stylus had been set up in addition to his regular laptop, each connected separately to a projector with feeding two screens. *This had better work, Eric,* Joe thought.

"Thanks to all of you for coming to what I hope will be a day of both reflection and revelation," Joe said. He had positioned himself in front of the podium rather than behind it. He knew that one of his strengths as a presenter was his physical presence. He tended to gesture and often, to pace. "And thanks to Michael, especially, for inviting me to speak. You'll have to forgive me if I'm a bit rusty – it's been some time since I had the chance to address a group as large as this one."

Joe cocked his head at a few empty tables, and there were some appreciative smiles. "I know you're probably ready to hit the buffet, as well," he continued. "So I'll get right to it."

On the left screen behind Joe, his first slide came up. It was an executive team of middle-aged Caucasian men.

"Leadership had its day," Joe said, pausing for effect as a giant X imposed over the picture, "But that day was yesterday." The room had become very quiet. He had their attention. "Yesterday, leaders focused on leading people and making money," he said. "Now, depending on your perspective (and possibly your age), that may sound like common sense. But after recently speaking with close friends and colleagues from a wide range of professions, reading and researching some of our best business minds, and reflecting on a management consulting career that spans 35 years travelling the globe, I've come to something of a revelation.

"If leadership is alive and well, why do so many great companies fail?" The screen to his left flashed images of company logos, including Polaroid, Kodak, Digital, Arthur Andersen, Eastern Airlines, Delta, PanAm, K-Mart, WorldCom, Nortel, Texaco, Lehman Brothers, Circuit City,

Blockbuster, Borders, Chrysler, and GM. As he spoke, Joe reached for his stylus and began to draw; three circles appeared on the screen to his right.

"In their heyday, these companies had satisfied employees, and were led by effective, and in some cases, extraordinary leaders. In most cases, they enjoyed exemplary cultures," Joe said, putting a check mark in each of the three circles in turn.

"But they either didn't survive, or had to be given CPR following bankruptcy." He turned to face the crowd head-on again. "Why? Well, I've concluded that profit, revenue growth, innovation, quality, customer satisfaction, and engaged employees, are all outcomes of something bigger.

"That something is Creativeship." He drew a fourth circle while dimming out the three circles he had sketched earlier. Meanwhile, on the left screen, his original leadership picture was replaced by a series of pictures representing the changing face of today's workforce semi-imposed over a map of the world. These included Boomers collaborating in open spaces, telecommuters working from their sofas, Millenials with Apple's signature white earbuds visible in their ears, employees texting at their desks, and working moms and dads holding babies while talking on mobile phones. All of these pictures were connected by straight and dotted lines. The distinctive logos of Facebook, Google+, LinkedIn, YouTube, and Twitter appeared among the photos, and subtle dotted lines zigged and zagged across the screen, indicating the connections these social networks enabled.

There was some shifting in the audience as his listeners exchanged glances and, in a few cases, leaned forward over their program binders and laptops. "I've often defined leadership as the ability to lead people, build fellowship, and make money," Joe continued. He cleared the tablet and quickly sketched a trash can. "But I've now chucked that definition," he said. "For me, it's gone the way of CD players, help wanted newspaper ads, corner video stores, and soon, I predict, the nine-to-five workday, job descriptions, and retirement plans." As he mentioned each of these topics, Joe drew arrows into the trash can. Finally, he circled the whole sketch and drew a line through it.

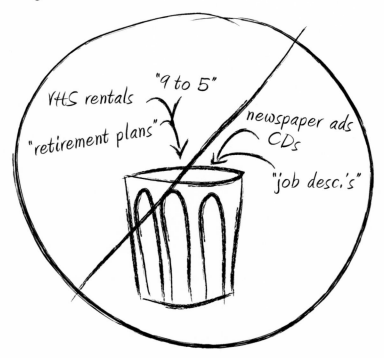

"So what has changed? And what is Creativeship?" Joe asked. "As I'm sure you've guessed, I've begun to develop a new definition." At a tap of the stylus, his sketch was replaced by the words:

CREATIVESHIP (n):

The Creation of Sustainainable Cultures and Business Models.

"Creativeship is a response to the unprecedented rate of change and diversity that characterizes our world and work," Joe said. "So many things are impacting business now to an extent and with a complexity that they haven't in the past. Technological advances. Globalization. Shifting economic drivers. Government intervention. Changing workforce demographics. Disparate motivational drivers with Generations X and Y. And the emergence of corporate social responsibility as an important characteristic of any organization."

He drew a wavy line under the word **Sustainable** in the Creativeship definition. "My thinking about this had a definite start date," he said. "It was during and following the collapse of the ENRONs, WorldComs, and Arthur Andersens of the world." Heads throughout the audience nodded. "We were all there," Joe said. "We saw what happens when firms become so singularly focused on profit that they lose their moral compass."

He used the Undo function on his tablet to erase everything from the screen but the word **CREATIVESHIP**, which he dragged to the center. (He was thanking his lucky stars for the impromptu training Eric had given him a month or so back on using the tablet, as well as for Eric's presence, and their many rehearsals.) "For firms to be sustainable, they need to invest their energies and resources in six prominent business priorities." Around **CREATIVESHIP**, he wrote:

Global Growth   Purpose   Engagement

CREATIVESHIP

Tri-Branding   Innovation   High Performance

"So let me address these in turn," Joe said. "Please note that they don't occur in any order; in fact, they overlap and intersect. I have become aware of the importance of all of them in a more or less continuous fashion – although there have been certain conversations and events in the last few years that really underscored certain aspects."

He circled the word **Purpose**. "This being an executive crowd, you've probably become familiar with mission statements. Some of you may have even had the, ahem, pleasure of having to help distill a company's 'what.' And you know that even getting that far can be a long, complicated process, especially if there are too many cooks involved," he winked. "But what I've come to see is that it's not sufficient to articulate 'what we do.' 'Why we do it' is equally, if not more, important. And that's what's known as an EVP: an Employer Value Proposition." He jotted **EVP** above **Purpose**.

"We're starting to see a real trend in socially conscious organizations outperforming ones whose implicit or explicit purpose is simply beating their competition in an economic sense. For example, we all understand what Whole Foods Market does." Here Joe pulled up a snapshot he'd taken of his neighborhood grocery. "They sell perishable consumer goods. Not to mention some pretty cool hats." He flipped to slide of Eric, adorned with a cozy, ear-flapped knit cap. He'd been captured looking a bit annoyed. The laughter that ran through the ground was invigorating to Joe. In row one, Eric rolled his eyes. (He'd tried to get Joe to use a different photo, but to no avail.) "But Whole Foods' purpose statement, or their 'why' is, 'To provide choices for nurturing the body, the community, and the planet.'

"Another example is Starbucks. We clearly know their 'what.' I see a few of you trying to hide your Venti Lattes right now! They sell premium coffee, and we all know it. But they have defined their employee value proposition – their 'why' – as, *To inspire and nurture the human spirit – one person, one cup, and one neighborhood at a time.*"

Joe saw a few among his audience armed with their own reusable coffee mugs looking a bit smug. He took the chance to assert, "Starbucks leadership also walks the talk. At the height of the recession in 2008, Starbucks' CEO, Howard Schultz, required that all 10,000 managers spend their first day of a leadership off-site volunteering to rebuild New Orleans after Hurricane Katrina."

He could see that some people had heard this story before, but a significant number looked surprised. "That might seem like the ultimate purpose-before-profit concession. But the point I'm trying to make is that the two drive each other. You can't expect that a sense of purpose will necessarily result from doing well financially with 'what you do.'

On the left screen, a split-screen slide with a twenty-something on one side and a man of about his own age on the other appeared. "Many of you may already be reaching information overload about Generation Y or Millenials," he said. "They've certainly been a focus of a great deal of media and scholarly attention in the past couple of years. The second demographic group getting attention lately is Baby Boomers, who will soon be taxing our Social Security system. But what you might not know is how much these two groups have in common." He gestured at the projected slide. "Millenials have been called the 'purpose generation.' But Boomers – that's me, and I think I see a few peers out there today – are increasingly leading corporate social responsibility efforts. In part this is because there are still so many of us in positions of leadership," he said, heading off a few skeptical looks from the crowd. "But a large part of the trend has to do with re-focusing on different priorities, after years of focusing on accumulating wealth and climbing the corporate ladder. You have to remember," he added, "that many Boomers remember the 60s and 70s, and many were involved or at least informed by the social causes that animated those decades." He flipped to a slide of the UC

Berkeley riot, and let that sink in for a moment before returning to his six key concepts

"So perhaps," Joe said in a quieter tone, "we shouldn't be surprised that this is a generation that has renewed efforts to push their employers to donate to charities and reduce their carbon footprint."

He now circled **Engagement**, and next to it wrote **200%**. "According to Gallup, companies with high engagement levels are 200% more profitable than their counterparts with low engagement levels," he said. "This is a reality that is starting to take hold, which I think is a good thing. Sources like Economic Intelligence, Aberdeen Group, and Pricewaterhouse Coopers are reporting things like employee engagement and talent management among the top concerns of the C-Suite."

He saved and cleared the screen, and wrote a large question mark in its center. "So, what's employee engagement, and how is that different from employee satisfaction?" he asked. He saw some eyes widen in the audience, and rushed to say, "First, in case you haven't heard the news: let me assure you that they are not the same thing. I define engagement as (he wrote while he was speaking):

The unlocking of employee potential to drive High Performance.

Joe drew a new wavy line under **High Performance**. "This is a pretty important distinction. And it's part of Creativeship, because you cannot have sustainable business cultures with employee satisfaction alone. Trust me: the last thing you want is a team of satisfied but underperforming employees!" With perfect timing, Eric brought up an image of a man with his sleeves rolled up and his feet up on his desk. The combination of the image and the last remark got the biggest laugh Joe had enjoyed so far. Clearly, many of the managers in this group had struggled with "employee satisfaction" before… and maybe a significant number had actually been the guy with his feet up at one point or another.

Joe cleared the screen and drew, for perhaps the hundredth time in his career, the three-circle Venn diagram he had used with Ed Burns. "Helping employees reach their potential requires that organizations capture the intrinsic motivational drivers of their employees, with the net result

being engagement and high performance," he said. "Author Dan Pink reinforces this message in his bestselling book, *Drive*." Here, he was on solid ground – obviously, this was one of the ideas that he'd cultivated throughout his career. But he wanted to make it clear that this was part of the necessary component – engagement – that infused Creativeship. So he spelled it out. "Creativeship is about developing a job match where you link what an employee is great at, what they love to do, and what needs to get done." On the left Eric brought up a generic image of a position description. A cannon blast sounded; on the left screen, the image shattered and fell away. Concurrently, on the right screen, a statement appeared: *"Creativeship will be about roles, not job descriptions. It's about valuing expertise, not years of experience. It's about giving people projects, not cementing them in functions."*

By this point, Joe was pleased to see, a number of people were taking notes, either on paper or on various devices. He moved on, returning to his handwritten circle of terms surrounding CREATIVESHIP. **Performance** was the term he circled next .

"This is one of the crucial areas of overlap," he said. "It's one of the reasons that my definition of engagement has high performance as a distinguishing characteristic. But for Creativeship to take hold, and for those sustainable business cultures to result, performance has to be a benchmark at both the individual and the company level. And that means commitment that goes both ways." Joe drew a stick figure, and then a cluster of stick figures, which he then circled. Between them, he drew a two-way arrow.

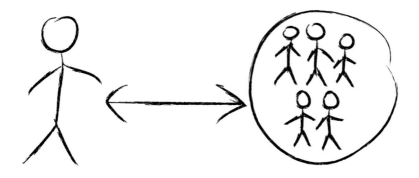

"The employee is accountable to the organization, and the organization to the employee. But that's old news." He drew a second two-way arrow over the first one. "The most important and tangible product of that commitment is performance," he said, drawing an asterisk over the second arrow. "And creating organization-wide recognition of performance as a goal that's arrived at mutually is key to Creativeship. The late Steve Jobs was adamant that Apple had to become a company of 'A-level performers' for Apple to be a sustainably great company. See, Steve knew that A players attract other A players."

Joe paused a moment for effect. Then he initiated an eye-catching, colorful fade effect that Eric had helped him create, which slowly replaced his last sketch with a picture of Joe that Heather had taken with her iPhone. His hair was mussed, and he was hard at work learning how to use the very tablet and stylus he was relying on for this presentation. He held up the stylus meaningfully as the audience took in what it was they were seeing, and was rewarded by a burst of laughter. Bringing the stylus slowly over the photo of himself for full effect, Joe wrote **Innovation**. He then added a question mark.

"As some of you may have gathered," he said, "and as my kids never tire of pointing out, I'm not usually the earliest adopter of new ways of doing things." A second wave of laughter succeeded the first. "But as you can see, an old dog can learn new tricks, given the right incentives. And I think we all know that business cultures that refuse to innovate, or even that put it off until it's too late, are undermining both engagement and sustainability. Almost by default, they stagnate. It's fun to speculate about the reasons that Polaroid didn't pursue digital photography, or why Digital Equipment Corp. continued to build mini-computers while startups were building personal computers. But ultimately it doesn't matter what those decisions were based on. We can learn from those failures – and the lesson is exactly what we all know it to be: *innovate or die*."

Joe drew a half-circle around the four concepts he'd addressed thus far.

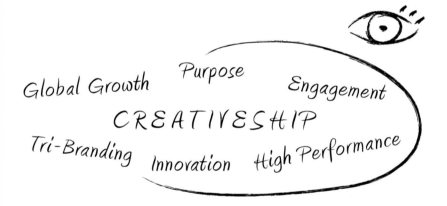

"**Innovation** underwrites all of Creativeship," he said. "It fuels **Purpose** and **Engagement**, and those two things drive **Performance**." In the top right of the screen, he drew an eye.

"But it requires better than 20/20 vision to achieve a culture of innovation," he warned. "I wasn't there, and I don't know exactly what the decisions were – but I'd be willing to wager that the bankrupted businesses I've cited today were a bit too focused on the short term. Creativeship requires investing today's cash to discover tomorrow's new technologies, products, services, geographies, and approaches. And I will be the first to admit that that may seem like a risk to a new, or even an established organization," Joe said. "But here's the kicker, and you can quote me on this." He advanced downstage and spoke in a theatrical whisper, flanking his lips with his hand. "It's way riskier not to do it."

He made a show of tiptoeing back to the podium, where he now circled the words **Tri-Branding**. His listeners' chuckles subsided as he resumed. "Branding has never been more important to a business. I'd like to show you something that I think is an excellent example of how leaders need to leverage and embrace branding as never before." On cue, Eric brought up a video on the left screen. Obviously an "amateur" work, it nonetheless had an appealing soundtrack and some eye-catching editing. In it, a small company offered potential recruits a walk-through of their office and interview process. The piece's very lack of slickness, including its use of real employees rather than actors, and hand-held footage that could have well been gathered on a phone, imparted an up-front, down-to-earth ambiance. Joe was not surprised to see smiles appear on many faces around the room.

"That was an entirely employee-generated film," he said. "The company held a contest to see who could best define its values and vision, with token gifts offered for the top five videos. Over the past year, this video has resided on the company's website and has become part of their outreach to new recruits. It's also on YouTube, where it has received over 130,000 hits.

"That," Joe said, "is what I've become accustomed to call 'co-branding.' Linking one's employment brand to one's service or product brand is an essential part of engagement, and the performance that results." He gestured toward **Engagement** and **Performance** on the screen, and then walked downstage again. "Here I should mention what a huge role social media has in all of this. Facebook, Twitter, and LinkedIn are just among the most established examples. Heck, I find myself hoping that some of you are tweeting about this gathering even as I speak," he joked, putting on his best stern father expression and surveying the crowd as he moved back to the podium.

"The thing I've come to realize about Creativeship – which we've defined as 'the creation of sustainable cultures and business models –' is that 'co-branding' is no longer enough." He cleared the screen and wrote **Organization** at the top. He then wrote **Employee** at the lower left, and **Customer** at the lower right.

"What we're really after is 'tri-branding,'" he said, drawing a triangle between the three words. "That's the magic that happens when companies build brand loyalty to the point where customers become brand ambassadors." He drew a series of lines radiating from **Customer**, connecting it to a host of small stick figures.

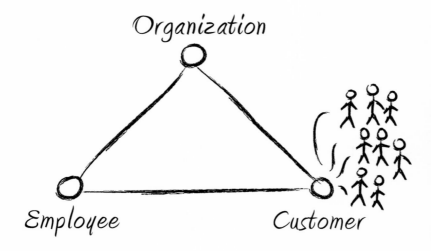

"Think BMW. They build cool products and hire people who are really interested in cars, especially sophisticated and technically advanced cars. BMW employees often drive BMWs themselves. That's co-branding." Joe gestured at the line connecting **Organization** and **Employee**. "The third dimension is the brand loyalty of their customers," he continued. "I know you know what I'm talking about. I think we've all seen BMW drivers on the road, and if you're like me, you hate them. I know, I'm one of them," Joe confessed to laughter. "BMW drivers become 'the ultimate driving machine' themselves. They live the product." About half of his listeners were smiling. A few were looking a little embarrassed, and a few, downright defiant. "Whatever you think of BMW personally," Joe said, "you can't deny that in a world where anyone can use social media to broadcast their likes and dislikes, engaging one's customers rather than just selling them a single product may be the distinguishing factor between the success or failure of a brand."

He flipped to a photo that Eric had taken of some bathroom graffiti. Among the expected crude notes and gang-style "tags" was a carefully drawn and instantly-recognizable

Nike logo. Joe paused a moment to let his audience absorb what they were seeing.

"Disregard for the moment that this is a bathroom on the Lower East Side," he said. "Think about how passionate you have to be about Nike to take the time to commit a minor act of vandalism that involves the company."

This was probably the most controversial image in his presentation, and Joe could hear a few feathers getting ruffled. He switched back to the word **CREATIVESHIP**, with its constellation of supporting terms, and redirected his audience's attention to **Tri-Branding.**

"I'd like to tell you a story that I hope you'll find amusing," he said. "Once upon a time, there were companies that put physical locks on rotary telephones so employees couldn't call their relatives or friends on the company's 800 number. Then there were companies whose legal departments were up in arms about giving employees access to email, because they were afraid that intellectual property would be at risk.

"But can you imagine doing business today without email? Without being able to phone whomever you wanted, whenever was convenient? I can't. And those two stories happened during my career, although I'm proud to say that I found them a little ridiculous even at the time."

He added a loop to his drawing, linking **Tri-Branding** with the other four concepts.

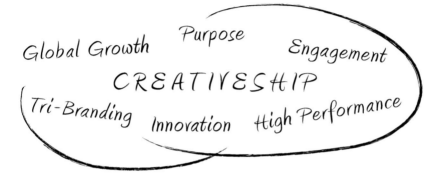

Global Growth   Purpose   Engagement
            CREATIVESHIP
Tri-Branding   Innovation   High Performance

"Social media is not going away, however much we may fear it," he said. "The smart thing to do – the Creativeship thing to do – is to embrace it as a branding opportunity, and to encourage your brand ambassadors, whether those are employees or customers, to make full use of it. This point was recently reinforced for me when I attended my son's college graduation. I looked out at the audience and saw what I thought were 3,000 small flashlights on the laps of the graduates. 'How thoughtful were the college organizers to supply flashlights to everybody so they can read the program,' I whispered to my daughter Heather." Joe paused a beat to deliver his punch line.

"My daughter replied, 'Dad, you idiot, those aren't flashlights. They're texting!'" The audience roared – it was easily the best laugh of the day. Joe continued, "Three thousand college graduates, all texting during the commencement address. That told me then and there, like it or not, social media is here to stay."

He was interrupted by a smattering of applause. Peering across the room, he saw that it was coming from a table of younger professionals that he would guess to be in their late twenties and early thirties. Rather taken aback, Joe nodded his appreciation. *In the home stretch now,* he thought. He had been so focused on delivering his message that he hadn't allowed himself to think about how he was doing. Nearing the conclusion of his presentation, he felt not just relief, but a certain amount of pride. His audience's response was letting him know that this hadn't been a waste of their time. *None of it's been wasted on my part, either,* Joe realized. *I've talked about purpose today; maybe this is mine!*

Suppressing a grin, Joe returned to his tablet and circled the words **Global Growth**.

"In many businesses, we've been accustomed to thinking about growth in a very limited way," he said. "For many of us, growth has meant either winning enough business to hire more people, or something more along the lines of mergers and acquisitions. But in a Creativeship environment, even those assumptions need to expand."

Next to **Global Growth**, Joe drew a brain. It didn't turn out quite as he'd liked, so he clarified, "That's meant to be a brain," to more laughter. "You have to have a growth mindset," he said. "I've already mentioned the adage, 'innovate or die.' Well, some of you may remember its origin as 'grow or die.' And the principle is much the same. It is a Creativeship mindset that doesn't see today's success as the place where you've crossed the finish line. The Creativeship mindset is, 'What's next?'"

He erased the brain he'd drawn. "Let's get rid of that," he said. "Apparently I need more practice. I'm better at circles," he said, drawing one and adding some rough approximations of continents.

Global Growth

"Globalization is key to growth. Companies who are local need to think regional; companies who are regional need to think national; companies who are national need to think global. As Thomas Friedman points out in *The World is Flat*, technology" – he pointed to the word **Innovation** and raised his eyebrows – "is creating a level playing field. Barriers are falling, with regards to both where you produce your product or perform your service, and in whom is producing or consuming it. And don't forget the co-branding aspect," he said. "Recent studies show that millenials are three times more motivated by career development opportunities than financial rewards, compared to older generations in the workforce." He wrote a large **3X** over the globe that he had drawn.

"I have three children of my own, all in very different fields," Joe said then. Eric transitioned the slide on the left to a photo of himself, Heather, and Stephen. "I'm very proud of all of them, but I think that any of you who are parents can relate to the vast difference between the way they think and the way we do." Just as at his retirement party, Joe was rewarded with some knowing looks from his own peer group. But the thirty-something table in the corner looked sympathetic, too. "I've been very grateful, especially recently, to have learned perhaps more from my kids than I did in the last few years when I was consulting. And one of the things I've learned is that for them, the world really is flat. They use technology all day, every day, to communicate with people around the world for both work and entertainment. It's second nature. And they want to work for companies that are on the same page – who think as globally as they do."

Switching back to his main Creativeship constellation, Joe looped the words **Global Growth** into the rest of the group, completing the family of concepts that made up Creativeship.

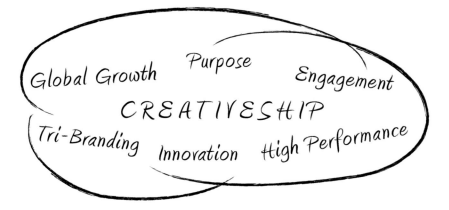

"So at the employee level, Creativeship is about creating cultures of personal growth and development, and about nurturing the idea of the company's purpose as a global one,"

he said. "But at the company level, it's about recognizing that you must invest in tomorrow, even if you're trying to avoid the ruts of today. When it seems that the clay of doing business is hardening, look for ways to re-mold it. Evolve, expand, or morph, but don't rest on your laurels. A stagnant culture is not a sustainable one."

He reset the image on the screen to his original Creativeship definition:

CREATIVESHIP (n):

The Creation of Sustainainable Cultures and Business Models.

"A lot has been written about the individual pillars I've talked about today: Purpose, Engagement, Performance, Innovation, Tri-Branding, and Global Growth," he said. "But it is their interdependence on each other that define Creativeship. You've got to create, and ask, 'What's next?'" he said. "Ask 'Why?' and 'Why not?' And don't take 'Because' as an answer."

He had delivered this last in a quieter tone. The audience seemed unsure whether he was quite finished. "Thank you," Joe said, clearing his throat. "Thanks for listening." He dipped his head and headed offstage.

The applause took a beat to begin, but Joe didn't think he was kidding himself that it was robust and sincere. He even heard a whistle, and was immediately sure it was the "kids" from the corner table. From offstage, he could see several in the audience getting to their feet while clapping. With a lump in his throat, Joe realized that his son was one of them. *Don't get misty, don't get misty…* he scolded himself. *Man, I hope I can get a recording of this,* he thought. *I'd love to show it to Heather and Stephen. Heck, maybe I ought to put it on YouTube, and see if I can get some more gigs like this one!*

"Great job, Joe," Michael Porter murmured as Joe passed him in the wings. "I'm sure there will be a lot of people who'll want to talk to you, and ask questions. You're going to stick around, right?"

"Oh yeah," Joe said, grinning. "I've decided to stick around." *More than you know,* he thought.

Key Learning
Take-Aways + Resources

PURPOSE

In Chapter 1, new retiree Joe
Daniels is beginning to take a hard
look at his career. This includes a
review of how the companies he's
served have succeeded, as well as
how they've fallen short. While
Joe and his daughter Heather
examine the crash-and-burn cycle
of certain real-life companies like
Enron, it appears that Joe's fictional
former employer ThinkSmart has
fallen prey to some destructive
impulses.

Joe's first Creativeship lesson is that a sincerely held and
concisely expressed sense of purpose is critical to an
organization's success. As a "Boomer," he and many of his
clients have been used to thinking of profit as the "end
zone." But over the course of the book, he will be assessing
the new business landscape with the lens provided by his
children and some younger colleagues, as well as further
reflecting on his life's experiences. Ultimately, Joe will realize
that profit is not sustainable long-term without employees
embracing a company's purpose, as leadership's evolution
towards Creativeship begins to crystallize in his mind.

Key Learning Points on Purpose:

- The implosion of companies like Enron and WorldCom, coupled with the global financial crisis of 2008, has sparked a global call for Corporate Social Responsibility (CSR) from employees, the media, government, and other key stakeholders.

- To best attract, hire, and retain the best employees, firms need to identify their employer value proposition (EVP), as a necessary step to promote their brand.

- Organizations must articulate not only "What we do," but crucially, "Why we do it." Success will increasingly depend on motivating existing staff and attracting new talent by positioning an organization as a "Purpose Employer."

- Socially conscious organizations, driven to improve the world, consistently outperform organizations solely committed to beating the competition (Logan, King, and Fischer-Wright, 2008).

- Driving home the importance of communicating purpose, 95% of the largest 250 companies of the world now report on their CSR activities (KPMG International Survey of Corporate Responsibility Reporting, 2011)

- The "Millennial/Generation Y" population, who comprise an overwhelming portion of new job candidates, are increasingly more focused on "purpose-driven" careers than paychecks. This is especially true in western nations where Boomer parents have succeeded in creating the world's wealthiest, most technologically savvy, and most globally aware generation of up-and-comers.

• Those who fall within the Boomer category are also finding renewed purpose in corporate social responsibility. Donations to charities, efforts to reduce corporate carbon footprints, and volunteer activities are at an all-time high with Boomers. Purpose is helping to bond coworkers of different generations. After years of focusing on wealth accumulation and climbing the corporate ladder, Boomers are now re-focusing their priorities and finding affinity with their younger cohorts in the workplace.

• Greed, while never an admirable trait, has never been less fashionable than today. Your employees, customers, candidates for employment, the government, media, and other key stakeholders now view greed as a corporate vice as well as a personal one.

Discussion Points on Purpose:

1. If companies had been more focused on purpose, could the 2008 financial crisis (considered by many economists to be the worst since the Great Depression) have been avoided?

2. Why did the ENRONs, WorldComs, and Arthur Andersens of the past decade lose their moral compasses? Could it have been prevented?

3. Why do some call Generation Y the "purpose generation?"

4. How can your business, department, agency, or school best define its "Why?"

5. How does purpose interdepend on engagement, high performance, innovation, tri-branding, and global growth?

Companies You May Know That "Get" Purpose:
- Whole Foods Market
- Timberland
- Warby Parker
- Starbucks
- Proctor & Gamble
- Target

...And A Few You May Not Know:
- Patagonia
- TOMS
- Mahindra Group (based in Mumbai, India)
- Beacon Communities
- BELL (Building Educational Leaders For Life)

CNN 2011 Rankings of Top Socially Responsible Employers:

- Statoil
- Ferrovial
- Walt Disney
- Edison
- ENI
- Whole Foods Market
- Total
- Hochtief
- Nestlé
- NextEra Energy
- Weyerhaeuser

Suggested Readings About Purpose:

- *Start With Why – How Great Leaders Inspire Everyone To Take Action.* Simon Sinek, 2011

- *The Power of Habit: Why We Do What We Do in Life and Business.* Charles Duhigg, 2012

- *A Whole New Mind.* Danel Pink, 2005

- *Purpose, The Starting Point for Great Companies.* Nikos Mourkogiannis and Roger Fisher, 2006

- *It's Not What You Sell, It's What You Stand For.* Roy M. Spence Jr. and Haley Rushing, 2009

- "How Great Companies Think Differently." Rosabeth Moss Kanter, *Harvard Business Review*, 2011

Suggested Videos About Purpose:

- "Drive: The Surprising Truth About What Motivates Us." Adapted from Daniel Pink's book by RSA Animate. youtube.com/watch?v=u6XAPnuFjJc

- "Start With Why." Simon Sinek, TEDx Puget Sound, 2009 youtube.com/watch?v=u4ZoJKF_VuA

- "If You've Never Failed, You've Never Lived." Bluefish TV, 2009. youtube.com/watch?v=2dbeJkY6QGk

Top Blogs Addressing Purpose:

- "David Coethica's Blog." David Coethica. davidcoethica.wordpress.com

- "Corporate and Responsible." Lucia Candu. www.corporateandresponsible.com

- "Crane and Matten Blog. Andrew Crane and Dirk Matten. craneandmatten.blogspot.com

- "FabianPatterg.com." Fabian Pattberg. www.fabianpattberg.com

- "MallenBaker." Mallen Baker, mallenbaker.net/csr/index.php

- "CSR-Reporting." Elaine Cohen. csr-reporting.blogspot.com/

- "CSR International." Wayne Visser.
csrinternational.blogspot.com/

- "The Business Ethics Blog." Chris MacDonald.
businessethicsblog.com/

- "Evolving Choice." Aaron Fu and Katherine Liew.
evolvingchoice.com/

EMPLOYEE ENGAGEMENT

At the party, Joe is surrounded by old colleagues, some of whom he remembers more fondly than others. Meanwhile, Heather is a bit perplexed by the difference Joe is trying to point out to her between "employee satisfaction" and "employee engagement." Joe stresses that satisfied employees are there to *get* while engaged employees are there to *give*. And while Joe makes an important point to his

EMPLOYEE ENGAGEMENT

daughter about fairness in pay or perks, he explains that long-term motivation (and a company's sustainability) come from something linked to Purpose: the desire to work for a winner.

This is a topic that Joe's old supervisor, Susan Delacourt, knows a lot about. He doesn't remember her as a particularly "nice" boss, but he has to admit that her fairness had been important to him. He also remembers that her division was among the highest-performing… and that, to paraphrase Susan, "winners want to work with other winners." Joe also admits that Susan's non-tolerance for mediocrity, insistence on holding people accountable, and instincts for communicating the organization's performance were vital in building the department's high-performing culture, although he found her somewhat overbearing at the time. Susan emphasizes that engagement begins at the hiring stage, and Joe recalls Susan's "B.E.S.T." principle. She claimed that people are often hired solely for aptitude with a focus on Education and Skills (the E and S in B.E.S.T.), but that true success comes from attitude, imbedded in Behaviors and Traits (the B and T).

Key Learning Points on Engagement:

*   Employee Engagement is all about *discretionary effort* – employees giving above and beyond because their commitment to the organization is reciprocated.

*   It's also about mutual commitment: the employer helping the employee reach his or her potential, and the employee helping the employer reach its business goals.

*   Employees often fall into one of two categories – those looking to give (engaged employees), and those looking to get (satisfied employees).

*   Engaged employees are driven to high performance.

*   Engaged employers reward and recognize success, and hold employees accountable.

*   Organizations that reward uneven performance equally with bonus distribution or raises (the "peanut butter" approach) risk discouraging high performers while disincentivizing underperformers from improving.

- Unless you are in a job where your behavior or demeanor is immediately rewarded, such as a waitperson or door attendant, pay is not a primary engagement driver. However, lack of equity can be a *disengagement* driver.

- Technology is a necessary engagement driver for younger generations. They expect to have the latest technological devices.

Discussion Points on Employee Engagement:

1. What can your team, business, department, agency, or school do to shift the focus from *satisfaction* to *engagement?*

2. If engagement starts at the top, how should your leadership team "walk the talk?"

3. How does engagement differ between generations? What are the different intrinsic motivational drivers for each generation?

4. How can you build mutual commitment between management and employees?

5. How does engagement interdepend on purpose, high performance, innovation, tri-branding, and global growth?

Companies You May Know That "Get" Engagement:

- Facebook
- Campbell's Soup
- Southwest Airlines
- Four Seasons Resorts
- Nordstroms
- Bain Consulting

... And A Few You May Not Know:

- Patagonia
- Momenta Pharmaceuticals
- Balfour Beatty Construction
- The Mentor Network
- VHB

Fortune Magazine 2012 Rankings of Best Employers:

1. Google
2. Boston Consulting Group
3. SAS Institute
4. Wegmans Food Markets
5. Edward Jones
6. NetApp
7. Camden Property Trust
8. Recreational Equipment, Inc. (REI)
9. CHG Healthcare Services
10. Quicken Loans

11. Zappos.com
12. Mercedes-Benz USA
13. DPR Construction
14. DreamWorks Animation
15. NuStar Energy
16. Kimpton Resturants & Hotels
17. JM Family Enterprises
18. Chesapeake Energy
19. Intuit
20. USAA

Suggested Readings About Engagement:

- *Louder Than Words: 10 Practical Employee Engagement Steps That Drive Results.* Bob Kelleher, 2010

- *Drive: The Surprising Truth About What Motivates Us.* Daniel Pink, 2011

- *Good to Great: Why Some Companies Make the Leap... and Others Don't.* Jim Collins, 2001

- *Strengths-Based Leadership,* Tom Rath and Barry Conchie. 2009

- *The Five Dysfunctions of a Team: A Leadership Fable.* Patrick Lencioni, 2002

- *Shackleton's Way: Leadership Lessons from the Great Antarctic Explorer.* Margot Morrell and Stephanie Capparell, 1998

- *It's Your Ship: Management Techniques from the Best Damn Ship in the Navy.* Michael Abrashoff, 2002

- *Fired Up or Burned Out.* Michael Lee Stallard, 2009

Suggested Videos About Engagement:
- "10 Steps of Employee Engagement." Bob Kelleher, youtube.com/watch?v=OHsB-cjyhzY

- "Drive: The Surprising Truth About What Motivates Us." Adapted from Daniel Pink's book by RSA Animate. youtube.com/watch?v=u6XAPnuFjJc

- "Harvard Business Review Case Study." Campbell Soup Company and former President and CEO, Doug Conant, is.gd/oKVwPC

- "Patagonia is a pioneer in the philosophy that created Will Marre's Giving is Winning List." is.gd/U9fADO

Top Blogs Addressing Engagement:
- "The Employee Engagement Group Blog." employeeengagement.com/news-blog/

- "Bloomberg Businessweek Employee Engagement Blog."
  http://is.gd/KejnVX

- "Society of Human Resource Management."
  blog.shrm.org/

- "Harvard Business Review."
  blogs.hbr.org/

- "TLNT: The Business of HR."
  tlnt.com/tag/hr-blog/

HIGH PERFORMANCE

Susan's lessons must have made more of an impression on Joe than he realized at the time. He recalls one instance where the high performance of a single member of his team could not outweigh an extremely poor attitude that was detrimental to the entire unit's engagement. Arrogant and brusque, Ed Burns tested Joe's patience to the limit, and despite his good contributions to the company's

bottom line, Joe was eventually forced to let him go.

So when Ed approaches him at the party, Joe is thrilled to learn that the younger man has come a tremendous way. He seems to have realized that his own unhappiness under Joe had to do with his own lack of motivation for all aspects of the job but one: winning the work. And while Ed may not recognize the extent to which his own lack of engagement was jeopardizing the group's performance, Joe begins to see Susan's point about their being a reciprocal relationship between them. Joe also recalls that the most motivated and high-performing employees are those who are in jobs they love, doing things they're great at, within the context of what has to get done.

Key Learning Points On High Performance

- "A-list" players want to work with other winners.

- It is critical to establish and communicate company, business unit, and individual performance benchmarks.

- A culture of high performance relates not only to performance standards (what someone does), but also to adherence to company values (how they behave or work within the company).

- High-performing companies realize that not holding low-performing employees accountable will erode engagement of high performing employees. Rewarding underperformance for the sake of equity is actually *unfair*.

- Successful companies use a benchmark of rewarding their "stars" with at least *twice* the bonuses and salary increases as they give their average employees.

- A high performing culture does not tolerate mediocrity. This may mean tenacity in corrective action and/or transition outside the company.

- If transitioning an underperforming employee, or an employee caught in a company downsizing, treat all outgoing employees with fairness, dignity, and respect. A company severance policy that is *better* than industry standards pays long-term "good will dividends".

- Encourage job rotation. Remaining in any job for a long period often results in complacency, deflating engagement, and stalling innovation.

- A true *team*, committed to high performance and working cohesively together, will always outperform a random group of "what's in it for me" individuals.

- To capture the intrinsic motivation of an employee, increase engagement while building high performance. Leaders should look to put people in positions where they love what they're doing, they're really good at it, and the work they're good at needs to get done.

Discussion Points on High Performance:

1. What can your business, department, agency, or school do to create a culture of high performance?

2. How can you best measure and reward individual performance while continuing to encourage teamwork and team goals?

3. What should your business, department, agency, or school do to balance the performance needs of today, with the investment needs for tomorrow?

4. "A players" want to work with other "A players." What should you do, specifically, to retain and attract high-performing employees?

5. How does high performance interdepend on purpose, engagement, innovation, tri-branding, and global growth?

Companies You May Know That "Get" High Performance*:

- Apple
- Google
- Amazon
- Coca-Cola
- IBM
- FedEx
- Berkshire Hathaway
- Starbucks
- Procter & Gamble
- Southwest Airlines
- McDonald's
- Johnson & Johnson
- Walt Disney
- BMW
- General Electric
- American Express
- Microsoft
- 3M
- Caterpillar
- Costco Wholesale

Fortune's 2012 list of 20 Most Admired Companies. These organizations historically outperform their respective peer groups.

... And A Few You May Not Know:

- Momenta Pharmaceuticals
- Beacon Communities
- Terracon
- NSTAR
- American Publication
- Boston Beer

Suggested Readings About High Performance:

- *Execution: The Discipline of Getting Things Done.* Larry Bossidy, Ram Charan, and Charles Burck, 2002

- *Coaching for Performance.* Sir John Whitmore, 2002

- *The Balanced Scorecard: Translating Strategy into Action.* Robert S. Kaplan and David P. Norton, 1996

- *The Goal.* Eliyahu M. Goldratt and Jeff Cox, 1992

- *Beyond Performance Management.* Jeremy Hope and Steve Player, 2012

- *Leadership Isn't for Cowards: How to Drive Performance by Challenging People and Confronting Problems.* Michael Staver, 2012

- *Seven Habits of Highly Effective People*, Stephen R. Covey, 2000

- *Winning: The Ultimate Business How-To Book.* Jack Welch and Suzy Welch, 2006

Top Blogs Addressing High Performance:

- "Closing the Intellegence Gap." David Cokins, blogs.sas.com/content/cokins/

- "Leaderchat." Ken Blanchard, leaderchat.org

- "Harvard Business Review." blogs.hbr.org/

- "tompeters!" Tom Peters. tompeters.com/

- "Business Blogs." businessblogshub.com/

- "Fast Company Blog." blog.fastcompany.com/

INNOVATION

As with the other conversations Joe has had the night of his retirement party, his talk with Ed Burns stimulates his thinking on another topic: innovation. In conjunction with purpose, innovation is the creative spark necessary to encourage open-ended questions such as "Why?" and perhaps more importantly, "Why Not?" The challenge Joe points out is the loss of creativity as we age: peaking at age 5, and sinking to its lowest point at age 44. How to retain creativity and innovation as companies age, grow, and lose nimbleness is a challenge all leadership teams face.

Joe points out that today's focus on short term results is like the farmer eating rather than planting his seeds. Taking the opportunity presented by a brief address to his guests, Joe talks about some companies that "get innovation," by maintaining their innovative pulse, and focusing on the long term. He is also sadly reminded of one that didn't: Deb Allen, a former client whose resistance to change sunk her organization's future. However, Deb seems rejuvenated by Joe's talk and eager to "talk technology" with Joe's daughter Heather.

Key Learning Points on Innovation:

- Creativity is the cornerstone of life. It keeps us vibrant and engaged, and empowers us to think differently. These are significant contributors to an organization's ongoing sustainability.

- Company policies are often in place to protect the many against the few who might abuse privileges. But if instituted or enforced in excess, they can suffocate creativity and empowerment, and over time, disengage employees. Company policies should be gateways, not obstacles, for creativity.

- Don't wait until your own retirement to start asking "why" and "why not." Productive questioning fuels innovation, which in turn fuels Creativeship.

- Companies that innovate look to run in their own race, rather than joining others' races.

- Research indicates that creativity is at its highest point in childhood, and declines throughout adulthood until retirement. So do laughter and question-asking, often resulting in "status quo" thinking that is not conducive to the innovation Creativeship needs to thrive.

- Technology is often key to innovation. It is also key to how younger people relate to their environment and to each other. If you resist embracing it, you do so at your own (or your organization's) risk.

- Short-term earnings (often magnified if a firm is publicly traded, or backed by venture capital or private equity) must be balanced against longer-term investment in new services, products, technologies, and geographies.

Companies You May Know That "Get" Innovation:
- Facebook
- GE
- Nike
- Proctor & Gamble
- Intuit

Discussion Points on Innovation:

1. What should your business, department, agency, or school do to create a culture of "Why Not?" and stamp out a culture of "Because?"

2. Patterning is a process of studying the innovative approaches, best practices, and processes from other industries and applying them to your own. For instance, if you're in the automotive industry, what can you learn from the hospitality, healthcare, E-commerce, professional services, or other unrelated industry that can help you innovate?

3. If you believe the adage "You get the behavior you measure," what measurements and reward systems can you put in place to encourage a culture of innovation?

4. Clayton Christensen's iconic business book *The Innovator's Dilemma* introduces the concept of disruptive innovation. What are you doing today to anticipate disruptive business models that can threaten your current business model?

5. How does innovation interdepend on purpose, engagement, high performance, tri-branding, and global growth?

... And A Few You May Not Know:

- Epocrates
- Momenta Pharmaceuticals
- Narayana Hrudayalaya Hospitals
- Southern New Hampshire University
- Double Negative
- Geocomp Corporation

Forbes 2012 Rankings of Top Innovative Companies:

1. Salesforce.com
2. Amazon
3. Intuitive Surgical
4. Tencent Holdings
5. Apple
6. Hindustan Unilever

7. Google
8. Natura Cosmeticos
9. Bharat Heavy Electricals
10. Monsanto
11. Reckitt Benckiser Group
12. Celgene
13. Nidec
14. Terumo
15. Infosys
16. Pernod Ricard
17. Keyence
18. FMC Technologies
19. Starbucks
20. Nintendo

Suggested Readings About Innovation:

- *The Innovator's Dilemma.* Clayton M. Christensen, 2011

- *The Innovator's DNA: Mastering the Five Skills of Disruptive Innovators.* Clayton M. Christensen, 2011

- *Innovation and Entrepreneurship.* Peter F. Drucker, 2006

- *What a Great Idea! 2.0: Unlocking Your Creativity in Business and in Life.* Chick Thompson, 2007

- *Steve Jobs.* Walter Isaacson, 2011

- *Switch: How to Change Things When Change is Hard.* Dan Heath and Chip Heath, 2010

- *The Myths of Innovation.* Scott Berkun, 2010

- *The Ten Faces of Innovation: IDEO's Strategies for Defeating the Devil's Advocate and Driving Creativity Throughout Your Organization.* Tom Kelley and Jonathan Littman, 2005

- *World Changers: 25 Entrepreneurs Who Changed Business as We Knew It.* John A. Byrne, 2011

- "Innovating in China's automotive market: an interview with GM China's president." McKinsey Quarterly, Glenn Leibowitz and Erik Roth, 2012

- "Who in Your Company Can Say 'Yes' to Innovation, Without Permission?" Harvard Business Review Blog Network, Vijau Govindarajan and Mark Sebell, 2012

Suggested Videos About Innovation:

- "Where Good Ideas Come From." Steven Johnson; youtube.com/watch?v=NugRZGDbPFU

- "The New Rules of Innovation." Carl Bass, CEO, Autodesk, TEDxBerkeley. youtube.com/watch?v=YKV3rhzvaC8

- "Innovation is Actually Easy!" Tom Peters. youtube.com/watch?v=8AGTpu_i8sc

Top Blogs Addressing Innovation:

- "Technology Review Feed - Tech Review Top Stories." technologyreview.com

- "Lateral Action." lateralaction.com

- "InformationWeek - All Stories And Blogs." informationweek.com/

- "scottberkun.com." scottberkun.com

- "Innovation Excellence." innovationexcellence.com/blog

- "Grant McCracken." cultureby.com/

- "Creative Think." blog.creativethink.com/

- "Mitch Ditkoff (Cofounder and President, Idea Champions)." ideachampions.com/weblogs/

- "Jeffrey Phillips (Senior Leader, OVO Innovation)." innovateonpurpose.blogspot.com/

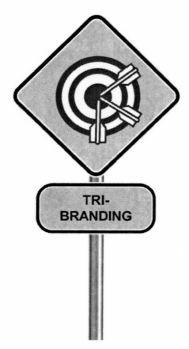

TRI-BRANDING

TRI-BRANDING

Joe has further opportunities to discuss Innovation with his party's caterer, Barbara… and with his daughter, Heather. Although she claims not to be as savvy as her younger brother, Joe is impressed by Heather's seemingly effortless multitasking between Twitter, Facebook, review-sharing sites like Yelp, and the real world. However, it is not just her ease with the Web on her iPhone that strikes Joe as being part of the idea he is developing. It is also the ease of immediately communicating opinions, good and bad, around the globe.

The phrase "brand acceleration" occurs to him. He recalls a campaign shortly before his retirement wherein the client was persuaded to forego more traditional means of advertising for a YouTube video campaign that went viral, with some excellent results for the company's brand. Where Joe has been used to think about "co-branding," where companies understand and promote their product brand and their employment brand together, he now adds a new "leg" to his concept: customers branding your product or service for you.

Key Learning Points on Tri-Branding:

- Co-branding is the connection between an organization's product/service brand and its employment brand.

- "Tri-branding" takes branding to a third dimension — leveraging external stakeholders as "brand ambassadors." External stakeholders include existing clients and customers, potential clients and customers, former employees, potential applicants for employment, vendors, media, and contacts within their physical or digital "communities."

- Client or customer satisfaction is passive/reactive ("Yes, I would use that company's service again." Or "Yes, I have shopped there.") Client or customer engagement is dynamic/proactive, where clients and customers go out of their way to refer a brand to others.

- Social media, combined with the connectivity provided by mobile devices, have become "brand accelerators," enabling propagation of memes (ideas, behavior, or style that spreads from person to person).

- Companies, restaurants, stores, and schools need to begin to regard everyone, from internal to external stakeholders, as potential brand ambassadors. By leveraging social media and mobile devices, an individual can now exponentially help (or hurt) a brand.

- Companies who embrace Creativeship crystalize their employer value proposition ("EVP") by defining "Why do people work here?" in order to maximize tri-branding potential.

- Companies with strong cultures hire employees whose behaviors and traits fit with the corporate culture to maximize the value of their EVP.

- To better understand whom to hire, organizations need to define the common attributes of the top 10% of their work force and/or to the common attributes of their most engaged employees. This provides insight into an employment brand by highlighting a common set of behaviors and traits that are collectively valued.

- The Internet and mobile devices have also changed the mechanism of "knowledge," if not its very definition. Yesterday, knowledge was power. Today and tomorrow, the *transfer of knowledge* is power.

Discussion Points on Tri-Branding:

1. Discuss all the reasons why your business, department, agency, or school does not embrace social media as a communication/alignment/branding vehicle. Now challenge yourself to ask "Why not?" each time the excuse begins with "Because," and prioritize ways you can leverage social media as a tri-branding tool.

2. Recently, it has been said that "Individuals are the brands of the future, not corporations." What does this mean? How does this relate to your job or career? Your employees? Your business?

3. What specific steps should you take to connect your product/service brand to your employment brand? Further, what should you start doing today to leverage your clients/customers as tri-brand ambassadors?

4. What specific competencies should you be looking for in future new hires to foster tri-branding connections and opportunities?

5. How does tri-branding interdepend on purpose, high performance, innovation, and global growth?

Companies You May Know That "Get" Tri-Branding:

- Southwest Airlines
- The TJX Companies
- BMW
- Hyundai
- Embassy Suites
- Apple
- Nordstrom
- Zappos

... And A Few You May Not Know:

- Warby Parker Eyewear
- In & Out Burgers
- Big Lots!
- Rent-A-Center
- Dunkin Donuts
- Zipcar

Suggested Readings About Tri-Branding:

- *Emotional Branding: The New Paradigm for Connecting Brands to People.* Marc Gobé. Updated and Revised Edition, 2010

- *Designing Brand Identity: An Essential Guide for the Whole Branding Team.* Alina Wheeler, 2009

- *Likeable Social Media: How to Delight Your Customers, Create an Irresistible Brand, and Be Generally Amazing on Facebook (And Other Social Networks).* Dave Kerpen, 2011

- *Content Rules: How to Create Killer Blogs, Podcasts, Videos, Ebooks, Webinars (and More) That Engage Customers and Ignite Your Business (New Rules Social Media Series).* Ann Handley and C.C. Chapman, 2010

- *The New Rules of Marketing & PR: How to Use Social Media, Online Video, Mobile Applications, Blogs, News Releases, and Viral Marketing to Reach Buyers Directly.* David Meerman Scott, 2011

- *Social Business By Design:Transformative Social Media Strategies for the Connected Company.* Dion Hinchcliffe, Peter Kim, and Jeff Dachis, 2012

Suggested Videos About Tri-Branding:
- "Did You Know 4.0." youtube.com/watch?v=6ILQrUrEWe8&feature=related

- "Name Branding 101." PacificRimStudios, youtube.com/watch?v=rVDgL_6glMg

- "Social Media Revolution 2012." youtube.com/watch?v=0eUeL3n7fDs&feature=related

Top Blogs Addressing Tri-Branding:
- "Brand Channel." brandchannel.com/home/

- "Branding and Marketing." brandandmarket.com/

- "Drew's Marketing Minute." drewsmarketingminute.com/

- "Danny Brown's Blog." dannybrown.me/blog/

- "Branding Strategy Insider." www.brandingstrategyinsider.com/

- "Marketing Profs." marketingprofs.com/

GLOBAL GROWTH

Toward the end of his drive to Heather's house, Joe muses not only about her ease with technology and about innovative technologies as "brand accelerators," but also about the need for generational diversity in the workplace if Creativeship is to take hold and thrive. Whereas Joe and many of his peers have tended to think of "Diversity" as the need for different ethnic and gender mixes in the workplace as a matter of compliance, after a restless night, he is convinced that it is more about cultivating superior ideas. *Diversity is as much about innovation and globalization as it is about equality*, he concludes.

The friends with whom he hits the golf green and clubhouse tend to agree. They themselves are a mix of different ages, genders, and backgrounds. As with the night before, Joe hears from several differing perspectives, and realizes that now more than ever, competition takes place on a global playing field. The creation of sustainable business cultures will not only result in global growth, he realizes, but it is ultimately dependent upon it.

Key Learning Points on Global Growth:

- Technology (i.e. internet, cellular communication devices, e-commerce, and mobile applications) is accelerating the globalization of both business and the workforce.

- Technology allows for a small company to compete on a global stage.

- Telecommuters are able to leverage technological advances to telecommute to work, regardless of what city, state, or country one may reside in.

- Previously, the motivation for a company to expand globally was to gain market share and/or gain access to cheaper labor pools. Companies must now look to expand internationally to win the 'war for talent.' Upcoming workforce demographic shifts will tilt the available labor pool from traditional western nations to developing nations, in particular, China, India, and Brazil.

- Today's younger generations are global, often spending time studying or living abroad and want to work for global employers.

- Diversity use to be about equality. Today, diversity is as much about diversity of thought, innovation, and globalization.

Discussion Points on Global Growth:

1. What are your human capital strategies to embrace global growth? Are you expatriating employees? If not, why not? Are you accepting of international transfers or new hires? If not, why not? Are you hiring employees with international experiences? If not, why not?

2. How can you best leverage technology to encourage global growth?

3. Discuss all of the ways you can expand your business model internationally? Include outsourcing, insourcing, telecommuting, acquisitions, mergers, partnerships, agents, relocation and transfer of employees.

4. What are your current clients/customers doing to grow globally?

5. How does global growth interdepend on purpose, engagement, high performance, innovation, and tri-branding?

Companies You May Know That "Get" Global Growth*:

1. Wal-Mart Stores
2. Royal Dutch Shell
3. Exxon Mobil
4. BP

5. Sinopec Group
6. China National Petroleum
7. State Grid
8. Toyota
9. Japan Post Holdings
10. Chevron
11. Total
12. ConocoPhillips
13. Volkswagen
14. AXA
15. Fannie Mae
16. General Electric
17. ING Group
18. Glencore International
19. Berkshire Hathaway
20. General Motors

* 2011 Fortune Global 500 top 20

... And A Few You May Not Know:

- SilkRoad Technologies
- AECOM
- Straumann
- Netapp
- SAS
- SC Johnson
- Diageo
- Medtronic
- Hilti
- Telefonica

Suggested Readings and Videos About Global Growth:

- *The World is Flat.* Thomas L. Friedman, 2005

- *A Whole New Mind: Why Right-Brainers Will Rule the Future.* Daniel H. Pink, 2006

- *Grow: How Ideals Power Growth and Profit at the World's Greatest Companies.* Jim Stengel, 2011

- *International Business: Strategy and the Multinational Company.* John B. Cullen, K. Praveen Parboteeah, 2009

- *Multinational Management.* John B. Cullen, 2010

- *What Chinese Want: Culture, Communism and the Modern Chinese Consumer.* Tom Doctoroff, 2012

- *That Used to Be Us: How America Fell Behind in the World It Invented and How We Can Come Back,* Thomas L. Friedman and Michael Mandelbaum, 2011

- "Did You Know? (Original.)" youtube.com/watch?v=xHWTLA8Wecl

- "Did You Know About The Future?/ Shift Happens – Globalization; Information Age." youtube.com/watch?v=XT_NyN0v60&feature=related

Top Blogs Addressing Global Growth:

- "The Economist." economist.com/blogs

- "Pankay Ghemawat." ghemawat.com/blog/

- "Harvard Business Review Blog." blogs.hbr.org/

- "Fast Company Blog." blog.fastcompany.com/

Creativeship Survey: How Do You Score?

THE CREATIVESHIP SURVEY

Is Creativeship present at your company? Take this easy survey and compare your results against the scale on page 199 to see how you stack up!

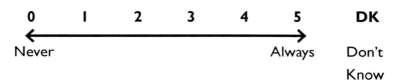

| 0 | 1 | 2 | 3 | 4 | 5 | DK |

Never   Always   Don't Know

1. We have a real commitment to high quality work, and tolerate nothing less.

   0   1   2   3   4   5   DK

2. Management gets the best work out of everybody.

   0   1   2   3   4   5   DK

3. We maintain a balance between short and long-term goals.

   0   1   2   3   4   5   DK

4. My company has a culture of diversity and inclusion – all employees are treated fairly regardless of age, culture, gender, race, thinking style, academic credentials, etc.

   0   1   2   3   4   5   DK

5. Promotions at my company are based on capability, not tenure.

   0   1   2   3   4   5   DK

6. The mission and purpose of this company make me feel that my job is important.

    0   I   2   3   4   5   DK

7. As a company, we routinely hire the best people.

    0   I   2   3   4   5   DK

8. I have the freedom to make the necessary decisions to do my work properly.

    0   I   2   3   4   5   DK

9. I am actively encouraged to volunteer new ideas and make suggestions for improvement of our business.

    0   I   2   3   4   5   DK

10. My company encourages global experiences.

    0   I   2   3   4   5   DK

Creativeship Survey Score

10-20 Minimal progress
(You have a pulse but need to ACT NOW!)

20-30 Marginally on your way
(But still BELOW Average!)

30-40 Middle of the pack
(Average, so there is HOPE!)

40-50 You're in the advanced class
(You're working for a LEADER!)

50 You can write the next book!
(You're BEST IN CLASS!)

Our Services

ENGAGE BOB TO SPEAK AT YOUR FIRM OR CONFERENCE!

Bob Kelleher is a sought-after speaker on employee engagement, workforce trends, leadership, and of course, Creativeship. Having spoken to hundreds of thousands of people at conferences and organizations all over the world, Bob's mix of humor, multi-media, case studies, and best practices have proven to be a winning formula for audiences across the globe. His high energy and always-current speeches are ideally suited for conferences, leadership offsites, and keynote presentations.

Visit www.BobKelleher.com for information on scheduling.

OFFERINGS OF THE EMPLOYEE ENGAGEMENT GROUP

Bob is CEO of The Employee Engagement Group, a global leader helping companies improve performance through enhanced employee engagement. Specific services include 90-minute, four-hour, eight-hour, and two-day workshops on topics including:

- **Creativeship.** This highly interactive workshop helps leadership teams build a sustainable organization by leveraging one or more of the themes explored in this book, including Purpose, Engagement, High Performance, Innovation, Tri-Branding, and Global Growth.

- **Engaging Employees To Drive Results.** Our signature workshop is a must for companies looking to elevate engagement by focusing on the "10 Steps of Engagement" as highlighted in Bob's best-selling book, *Louder Than Words*. A tried and true game changer for anyone who manages people.

- **Additional Workshops.** These cover topics such as performance management, change management, innovation, leading different generations, and employment branding, among others.

Employee Engagement and Creativeship Surveys

The Employee Engagement Group's powerful, cost-effective employee engagement and Creativeship surveys include outstanding benchmark norms, along with knowledge to help you with data interpretation, prioritization, and action planning.

Engage On Demand Resource Library

Membership in The Employee Engagement Group's "Engage On Demand" library is the industry's first cloud-based

resource, offering clients unlimited access and use of "best
in class" organizational development tools, training, and
templates. Best of all, what clients use, they own. FOREVER!

Most consultancies help companies decide *what to do*. We
also want to teach our clients *how to do it* by offering them
online access to this extensive library of world-class talent
management tools.

To Order More Books

Both this volume and Bob's *Louder Than
Words: Ten Employee Engagement Steps
That Drive Results* are available online at
Amazon.com, BarnesandNoble.com, or
EmployeeEngagement.com.

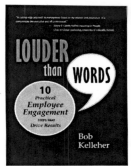

Visit www.EmployeeEngagement.com
for more information about any of our group's offerings. We
look forward to hearing from you.

Drop me a line at rkelleher@employeeengagement.com to
tell me what you thought of this book, share additional best
practices, invite me to speak to your leadership team, or simply
to say hello. You can also follow me on twitter @BobKelleher.

—

CPSIA information can be obtained at www.ICGtesting.com
Printed in the USA
BVOW032201101012

302593BV00001B/7/P

9 780984 532919